'POEM JENNY'

This etching entitled 'Lawn Market from above the West Bow' by Walter Geikie (1795-1837), showing a woman 'chaunting' from a broadside, is reproduced from his 'Proof Etchings' published in the 1860s. Janet Reid sold her broadsides in Edinburgh too – but the first time she did this was in 1840 which was three years after the death of Walter Geikie.

'POEM JENNY'

Janet Reid (1777-1854) of Carnock & Bridge of Allan, Scotland

On discovering the 'unpolished' poems of a forgotten 'poetess'

Against me, some people has a clamour,
For in my little poems, there is no grammar –
Such reek as in the house must come out at the lum –
My little unpolished poems does please some.

Janet Reid – On Edinburgh City

Edited by David A. Flint

HALF DOME

First edition 2015

Published by Half Dome
HD
30 Barn Lane, Oakley, Basingstoke, Hampshire
RG23 7HT
davidaflint@btinternet.com

A CIP data record for this title is available
from the British Library.

ISBN 0-9538513-2-X

Designed and word-processed by David A. Flint

Printed and bound by the Catford Print Centre
3 Bellingham Road, Catford,
London SE6 2PN

CONTENTS

The picture of the Airthrey Well House and its Pump Room, Bridge of Allan, on the cover of this book is reproduced from a hand-coloured print probably dating from the 1840s by an unknown artist. It was bought by J. Malcolm Allan from Bridge of Allan Books. The Mine House is glimpsed on the extreme right of the scene and the Bath House is behind the artist. Could the woman wearing a shawl on the right of the foreground group be Janet Reid selling a broadside to a family of a mother, daughter and son? It would be natural for the artist to include a typical foreground group – and Janet Reid was constantly at the Airthrey Well House when it was open from 1841 to 1854. Perhaps this is a drawing of Janet Reid!

It would seem desirable that Janet's poems should be given in chronological order. This might show her development as a poet (it does not); or it may shed light on her life (it does). Additional details of the historical allusions in each of Janet Reid's poems which help to date them or the contemporary background to the poems can be found in the NOTES.

The broadsides are reproduced at about two-thirds their actual size.

DEDICATION

Leslie Shepard in *The History of Street Literature* (1973) explains why so few broadsides have survived:

> In the nineteenth century there was a final tremendous outpouring of every kind of street literature, just before the introduction of cheap books and newspapers. Thousands upon thousands of broadsides and chapbooks swept like a tidal wave over the streets and market-places. And as the tide receded, much of this fragile ephemera disappeared, leaving only the souvenirs secured by thoughtful collectors.
>
> *Leslie Shepard*

This book is dedicated to the 'thoughtful collectors',
some known, others unknown, of
Janet Reid's broadsides
and chapbook

EPIGRAPHS

This was done by one who never was at school.
Janet Reid – On Children Going to Church

When I was young, a boy of me did take great care,
And learned me to read when he had time to spare.
Janet Reid – On the Jolly Tailors

For the Farmers I hae always had great respect –
For my welfare in former years they did not neglect.
Janet Reid – On the Farmers

I'm not now able the harvest for to shear;
I thank the public for many a penny and half-penny to me they do spare.
Janet Reid – On the Mid-Mill

For my uneven lines you will excuse,
For the pen, that valuable thing, I was never learned to use.
Thanks to the youths that my poems did write,
Although I sat by them and to them did dite.
Janet Reid – On Edinburgh City

I've travelled in Glasgow through many a street.
And the people in Glasgow to me were always discreet.
Janet Reid – On Glasgow's Bonny City

Now I have taken a habitation in the west countrie,
And the people there is very kind to me.
Janet Reid – On the Distress of the Working Classes

Marriage is only for this life,
And it's not ordained for every woman to be a wife.
Janet Reid – On Airthrey Water

ON THE GALLANT SAILORS.

The carpenters make the ships both firm and stout,
And to the seas the sailors with them most steer about,
If it were not for the sailors we would never get a cup of tea,
Nor as little a pound of sugar to sweeten it wi',
Nor as little people would get tobacco nor snuff,
Nor as little would the ladies get a silk gown or a muff,
And many other good articles I need not mention,
For carpenters to build ships it was a good invention,
I hope sailors will be men that will not be idle,
And when they are upon the seas I hope they'll read their
Bible.
They will mind how Jesus to Peter stretched out his hand,
It was upon the seas, it was not upon land.
They will remember how Christ taught out of a ship,
And never let true religion out of their mind slip,
I hope sailors will always believe on God's beloved Son,
For with both sea and land we will soon be done.
Every well-thinking person for sailors would pray,
For their lawful calling makes them in danger every day.
That pleasant beloved minister, Mr Brand,
Often prayed for them that was far from land.
When sailors leave their friends at home,
I hope they'll be mindful of them when to sea they're gone.
I hope people will mind when Jonah out of the fish did pray,
Both by sea and land make God our all-sufficient stay.
Now you carpenters and sailors I bid you all adieu,
I wish God's blessing may be always with you,
Read Boston and Wilson and William Dyer,
Of these three authors I think you'll never tire.

JANET REID, *Carnock.*

Peter Forbes' album.

[*No printer's imprint – possibly printed in Kirkcaldy, 1840*]

[*See the poem on page 51*]

ON JANET REID

THE MARRIAGE of John Reid and Janet Malcolm and the birth of their daughters, Janet and her younger sister Helen, in Saline (2 miles north of Carnock and 5 miles west of Dunfermline), Fife, Scotland, are recorded in the Old Parish Register of Saline:

November 29th: [1776]	*Reid & Malcolm. John Reid and Janet Malcolm both in this parish inlisted their names and after the usual proclamations were married Dec. 27th* [*1776*].
November 9th: [1777]	*John Reid weaver in Sandydub and Janet Malcolm B*[*irth*]. *Janet Law*[*fully*]. [*and baptism on*] *16th* [*1777*] *in presence of the Congregation.*
March [1781]:	*John Reid weaver in Sandydub and Janet Malcolm B*[*irth*]. *Helen, March 18th* [*1781*] *Law*[*fully*]. [*and baptism on the same day*] *before the Congregation.*

The first Ordnance Survey map of 1856 shows that Sandydub was the farmhouse that is now named Shieldbank Farm lying one mile north-east of Saline on the minor road to Dollar.

Janet Reid was never sent to school. Ability to read was widespread in Scotland at this time and being unable to read was thought shameful so children who had not been taught to read at school often learnt at home (like Janet) or as adults. However, being unable to write (like Janet) was not viewed in the same way. She had to earn her living as an 'agricultural labourer' from an early age.

The Old Parish Register of Saline records that a Janet Malcolm (who may have been Janet Reid's mother) died in 1785 when Janet was aged 8. The Old Parish Register of Saline also records that a Helen Reid married George Wishart in Saline in 1820; and the Old Parish Register of Dunfermline shows that a Helen Reid and George Wishart of Dunfermline had a daughter named Janet born in 1821 who died aged 11 in 1833. In Scotland, the first daughter was normally named after the mother's mother so, possibly, Janet Reid's mother died when she was a child and she once had a niece.

Sixteen years after Janet Reid's death in 1854 a poem by Edith McAlpine of Limekilns (a village on the Firth of Forth 3 miles south of Dunfermline) was printed in the *The Dunfermline Saturday Press & West of Fife Advertiser* on 3 September 1870. I found this in the British Library Newspaper Archive, Colinton, North London:

> Edith McAlpine, Limekilns, desirous of rescuing the memory of Janet Reid, the Saline carrier, from oblivion, sends us the following 'In Memorium' for insertion in the 'Poets' Corner'. The race of peripatetic carriers is now nearly extinct, but it formerly numbered in its ranks many noted worthies of both sexes. Not the least remarkable of these, perhaps, was old Janet Reid, who for many years acted the part of foot-carrier to the people of Carnock and Saline. It need scarcely be said that Janet knew everybody and everything that took place in the countryside, and was consequently a great favourite with the gossips, who, but for her, and when papers were scarce, would never have been posted up in the 'Latest News'. Janet was a good example of her race [kind] – strong, healthy, cheerful, and obliging. But Janet was more than all this – she was a poet in her way; and if facility of versification, readiness of wit, and an occasional touch of satire, were any proof of her ability in that line, then she must be pronounced a good one indeed. Carnock at present boasts of a poet, but old Janet could boast of a prior claim to the title of 'Carnock Poet', although her effusions have probably never yet been embalmed in printers' ink.
>
> By the way, one of the oldest survivors of the race still travels daily between Limekilns and Dunfermline. 'Auld Jenny' – for it so happens that she is a Jenny also [so Janet Reid was known as 'Jenny', a diminutive used in Scotland for 'Janet'] – may be seen in all weathers trudging along on her daily journey, with a load on her back that would put to shame many a stalwart youth of less than a third of her age. Strong, healthy, cheerful, and uncomplaining, it is always a pleasure to meet her honest countenance, and receive her hearty greeting as she trudges along; and though she has never cultivated the poetic muse like old Janet Reid, her kindly face, we are sure, would be none the less missed were she unfortunately laid aside from 'public duty'. Without further comment, we append the lines on the 'first Carnock poet':

'Poem Jenny'

IN MEMORIUM

When Janet she was young an' stour*, [energetic]
Grim poverty ne'er reached her door,
She ne'er got rich, but wasna* poor; [was not]
Aye* keen to learn [Ever]
Some honest shifts, that she might try
Her bread to earn.

Her place of residence an' dwellin'
Was in a wee* cot-house in Saline, [little]
To carry parcels was her callin',
    Sometimes a letter,
She got a penny for the piece –
    They paid her better.

[So Janet worked as a 'foot-carrier' before she left Saline]

So trim as she gaed* toddlin' doon, [went]
Awa'* for errands to the toon; [Away]
So neatly killet* was her goon*, [pleated, gown]
    Baith snod an' braw*; [Both neat and fine]
A petticoat* o' crimson hue, [skirt]
    Smock white as snaw*. [snow]

Her mutch* it was a clean sawback, [linen cap]
To mak' it pure she wasna slack;
The burden-sheet upon her back
    Was aye sae* clean, [so]
It might hae* graced the marriage-bed [have]
    O' ony* Queen. [Of any]

So smart, so blithesome, licht, an airy*, [cheerful]
She took the road swift as a fairy;
While money* a parcel she did carry, [many]
    For bawbees* little; [coins]
To earn a' honest livelihood
    Was very kittle*. [adept]

Continued

An' often comin' frae* the toon [from]
At nicht*, after the sun gaed doon*, [night, goes down]
She ne'er was fear'd for ony loon*, [any rascal]
        Or yet the Devil;
A free an' honest heart always
        Kept her frae* evil. [from]

She ne'er gave way to superstition,
She dreaded nae* unearthly vision, [no]
But aye* was pleased wi' her condition, [ever]
        An' trudged awa*, [away]
Whiles wadlin' ankle an' knee-deep
        Amang* the snaw. [Among]

Although her heart was aye alowe*, [always aglow]
Sly Time plough'd furrows on her brow,
An' shap'd her frame wi' Nature's bow;
        Then she resign'd,
An' left her callin' for some other
        To come behind.

She didna* mean tae sit forlorn, [did not]
But planted doon near the hawthorn*, [Thorn Cross]
In Carnock, where she micht* adorn [might]
        Her sex an' race*, [kind]
An' kindle burnin' lichts* to shine [lights]
        Aboot that place.

[The 'Thorn Cross' in Carnock was a 300-year old hawthorn tree surrounded by stone steps (removed in 1840) which were probably the base of a stone cross that was torn down in 1560 at the time of the Reformation and replaced by the hawthorn tree.]

The Scriptures from her lips did flow,
Infuse'd wi'* rich poetic glow; [with]
It wasna for a gandy* show, [boastful]
        But juist* tae win [just]
The hearts o' everyone, before
        Her glass was run.

Though high enlighten'd poets rise –
Minds swell'd wi' knowledge bricht* an' wise, [bright]
Like glitterin' stars the world surprise –
'Twill ne'er be hid,
Those brilliant lichts were made to shine
By Janet Reid.

Edith McAlpine, Limekilns

The only broadside that I found of *On the Mid-Mill* (see page 54) by Janet Reid has a pencil note written at its foot: '*See other side*'. Written there in ancient pen and ink is this description:

> *Janet Reid is 63. First beginning of her poetry was about four years since when some of her neighbours were wishing to give a coat to the Bellman – a young man had written the Subscription paper & after she had got subscriptions the young man took away the paper again & the old man did not get his coat – Janet was angry at this & made a copy of verses on him – & recited it to the neighbours in revenge – they approved of it & urged her to do more & once Captain Wemyss who the Carnock folk wanted to be made a Parliament man and on whom she had made a long poem sent her a pound. This encouraged her to go on altho' she thought shame of it at first – she cannot write but her neighbours write her verses for her. Was born in Salon near Carnock in the West Neuk of Fyfe – has lived in Carnock 15 years.*
>
> *19 Sept 1840*

There is an 'East Neuk [Corner] of Fife' and a 'West of Fife' – but the 'West Neuk of Fife' is the contrary notion of Janet Reid.

Janet must have told this story to the buyer of the broadside. From her poem *On Pretty Paisley*, Janet can be deduced to have been in Paisley on 19 September 1840. 'Salon' (spoken with Janet's Fife accent) is Saline. So Janet moved to Carnock in 1825 and she began composing poems in 1836. Perhaps Janet's father died in 1825 and this forced her to move. Captain James Erskine Wemyss RN. sat as the Liberal Member of Parliament for the County of Fife between 1820 and 1847 and he was re-elected in 1835 and 1837.

At first Janet Reid would have had her poems printed as broadsides in Dunfermline though none have been found printed there. She would have sold them on the streets and from door-to-door.

The Stirling architect John Allan (1847-1922) compiled *Carnock: Ancient and Modern, and Village Life* which was published in 1895. He comments: 'The dialect of the parish is that of a primitive, quaint simplicity, which the educational deluge has not yet obliterated'. This reflects the view of the Rev. Alexander Thomson (minister of Carnock) who reports in *The 'Old' Statistical Account of Scotland* (compiled 1791-99) that: 'The language now spoken in this district is the broad Scottish dialect with the Fifeshire accent which gives some words so peculiar a turn as to render the speaker almost unintelligible to the natives of a different county'.

Lizz Mogg of Carnock spotted this anonymous, untitled poem (composed in the 1860s) quoted by John Allan in 1895:

Dwelt in Carno', poem Jenny,
Who clinked* the line, turned* the penny; [rhymed, earned]
Across the ford cam' Muckle* Jock, [came Big]
To ply the flail, hooch, thrash* the stock; [thresh]
At Cairney liv'd a gentle colt*, [idle young man]
Who whig'd his whiggle*, screw'd his bolt*; [idled, did little]
Car's Pastor thump'd*, cam' doon pell-mell; [preached loudly]
The Dom'nie* sat accus'd himsel. [School-master]
The Bethel's* e'e revealed the wine, [Beadle's eye]
And flush'd Mactak, who nipt the coin*; [collected offering]
Rang* kirk and fair, wi' the guller*, [Roared, gossip]
Mill and smid'* o' Mudie's suller *, [smith's forge, Money]
The Laird who pu'd doon hus'* an ha'*, [pulled down house, hall]
An 'Little Jack' who shot the craw*, [ran away]
Mouter*, malter*, souter*, ploughboy, [Miller, brewer, cobbler]
Have had their day carouse and joy.
Then Oakley bellow'd, belch'd, and bock'd*, [vomited]
And collier* curs'd, and fought, and smok'd; [coal miner]
The Pastor took his pinch o' snuff,
At times a dram*, at times enough. [glass of whiskey]
And so auld things have pass'd away,
To be dressed up another way.

'Carno' or 'Car' is the village Carnock and 'Cairney' is Cairneyhill a neighbouring village – and 'poem Jenny' is Janet Reid. Oakley village was built for the miners of coal and iron-ore for the Forth Iron Works which opened near Carnock in 1846 and closed in 1869.

Janet's journeys can be deduced from her poems and her broadsides. She probably first made a visit to Kirkcaldy, Fife, in 1839 and returned to Carnock. She left Carnock sometime in 1840 after composing her poem *On the Mid-Mill* (near Dunfermline) in which she says: 'Ere ever the year 'Forty comes round again' but before composing *On Glasgow, Bonny Town* which ends: 'My Glasgow friends, this was written in the year Eighteen-Forty for you'.

Why did Janet Reid leave Carnock in 1840? The Rev. William Gilston in *The (New) Statistical Account of Scotland* (compiled 1834-45) writes that a daily penny-post carriage began between Carnock and Dunfermline in 1838. So a foot-carrier would no longer be needed (though Janet may have stopped doing this) and she probably found it difficult to earn a living by selling her broadsides in her locality. This is how she appears to have travelled:

1777-1825: Saline – Dunfermline – Saline.
1825-1836: Carnock – Dunfermline – Carnock.
1836-1838: Carnock – Dunfermline – Saline – Torryburn –
– Carnock.
1839: Carnock – Dunfermline – Kirkcaldy? – Carnock.
1840: Carnock – Edinburgh – Glasgow – Paisley – Glasgow –
– Kirkintilloch? – Falkirk? –
1841: Falkirk? – Stirling – Bridge of Allan – Dunblane –
– Torryburn – Carnock – Glasgow –
1842: Glasgow – Paisley – Glasgow – Stirling –
– Bridge of Allan – Glasgow –
1843: Glasgow – Paisley – Glasgow – Edinburgh – Stirling –
– Bridge of Allan – Edinburgh –
1844: Edinburgh – Glasgow – Paisley – Glasgow – Stirling –
– Bridge of Allan.
1845: Bridge of Allan.
1846: Bridge of Allan – Torryburn? – Carnock – Bridge of Allan.
1847-1854: Bridge of Allan.

Janet Reid may also have visited other places or may have made more moves. Janet would have had an annual pedlar's licence. Since 1696 pedlars (vendors on foot) and hawkers (vendors with a cart or a horse and cart) needed a licence costing £4 annually; and from 1810 pedlars or hawkers also needed a certificate signed by a local clergyman and two reputable inhabitants of the parish in which they lived stating that they were fit to hold a pedlar's licence.

Janet appears to have put her home on her broadsides as 'Carnock' at first – as put on the broadside of her 'New Year' poem *On the Year 1841*; then as 'Carnock, Fifeshire' from late in 1842 – as put on the broadside of her poem *For the New-Year* (1843); and then as 'Bridge of Allan' from late in 1843 – as put on the broadside of her 'New Year' poem *On the Year 1844*. Janet finally settled in Bridge of Allan during 1844 when the Airthrey Well House opened for the whole year instead of only from April to the end of September.

But she first visited Bridge of Allan in 1841 which she confirms in her poem *On the Bonny Alley Tree*. The population of Bridge of Allan was small at that time but an increasing number of visitors were coming to visit the Airthrey Well House. After 1841 Janet spent from April to September in Bridge of Allan and the winters of 1841-42 and 1842-43 and 1843-44 in Edinburgh or Glasgow. When the Well House opened all the year round from 1844 she was able to earn her living all the year round in Bridge of Allan.

In the national census taken on the night of 6-7 June 1841, Janet is probably the 'Janet Reid' recorded as born in the county, age 60 (she was aged 63 but ages were rounded down to the nearest 5 years) living with John Hunter an 'agricultural labourer' and his wife Helen Cochrane in Torryburn, Fife, 2 miles south of Carnock. Janet had evidently returned to Carnock to sell her broadsides at the Carnock Fair held annually on the 26 May. She did this again in 1846.

Janet Reid is living on the 'High Road (the Turnpike Road)' now Henderson Street in Bridge of Allan in the parish of Logie in the national census held on the night of 30-31 March 1851. She is a 'visitor' lodging with James Kepson aged 49 an 'agricultural labourer' and his wife Margaret aged 46 and their children George aged 16 and John aged 7. Janet Reid is shown as unmarried, aged 73, with the occupation of 'poetess' and as born in Saline, Fife.

The censuses of 1841 and 1851 in the parish of Logie also record a Thomas Reid born in Saline, Fife. In 1851 he is aged 43 and a 'fishmonger' living in Rose Street (which no longer exists) in Bridge of Allan with his wife Janet aged 48 and their sons Robert aged 19 and William aged 15. Perhaps they were the 'relatives' to whom Janet Reid left her savings when she died.

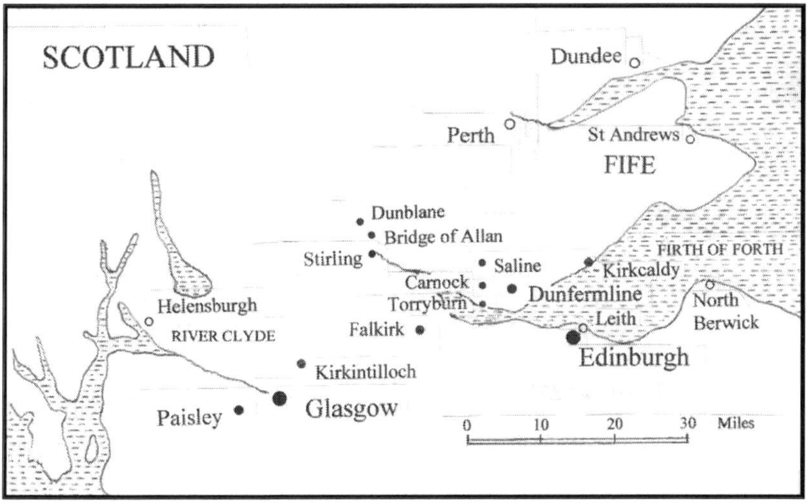

The places in Central Scotland that Janet Reid visited, or may be reasoned to have visited, are shown by black circles.

I found Peter Forbes' album in 1998 at the closing-down sale of D.M. Beach's antiquarian and second-hand bookshop in Salisbury, Wiltshire. It was entitled *Rhymes by Janet Reid, Carnock*, bound in half-leather and marbled boards and it contained 35 broadsides mounted on leaves watermarked 1805 and 1806. Virginia Wills of 'Bridge of Allan Books' put me in touch with J. Malcolm Allan, the Rare Books Librarian at the University of Strathclyde, Glasgow, and archivist of the Dr William Halliday Welsh Educational and Historical Trust in Bridge of Allan. The two weekly newspapers published in Stirling in the 1800s have been indexed and he spotted two entries made for 'Reid, Janet of Bridge of Allan: Poetess' in *The Stirling Observer Index: People 1836-1856* published by Stirling District Libraries in 1988. The first entry was printed in *The Stirling Observer* on 25 June 1846 under the heading 'Original Poetry':

JANET REID
The Bridge of Allan Poetess

A'* ye by braes* of Bridge of Allan, [All, hills]
What's this that now has you befallen?
I rede* ye a', baith* man an' callan'*, [advise, both, lad]
To tak' gude* heed — [good]
Ane kent* in Highland glen an' lawlan' [One known]
Is Janet Reid.

Douce* Janet weilds a pithy pen, [Respectable]
A ten-horse-power o' critic men,
There's nought o' ill within her ken* [knowledge]
But shaws* the deed — [shows]
She hurls back mischief to its den —
Bauld* Janet Reid. [Bold]

Wi' Landon's taste, and Heman's power,
Or Dante's dark Satanic lower,
She mak's even infancy to cower
Wi' shrinkin' dread —
Keen satire fa's* in heavy shower [falls]
Frae* Janet Reid. [From]

Nae coaches now on Sundays run —
That triumph honest Janet's won —
The coaching trade is a' but done,
'Tween this and Tweed:
Nane* shoots wi' sic* a killin' gun [None, such]
As Janet Reid.

Philp leaves the new hotel, 'tis said,
And Barr has ta'en his weary bed —
Nae horse to stable now is led
To get his feed —
And e'en the tollman now is fled:
Thanks! Janet Reid.

[Robert Philp and Matthew Barr were hotel-keepers in Bridge of Allan]

Nae droskies* now drive to Blawlowan, [carriages]
To crush the lily or the gowan* — [daisy]
Gig wheels nae mair* our streets are ploughin' [more]
At railway speed —
The grass on ilka* highway's growin' [every]
Bless! Janet Reid.

Her verse is o' that kindlin'* kind, [congenial]
That speaks alike to heart and mind —
The chiel*, indeed, maun* e'en be blind, [fellow, must]
Past a' remead*, [all remedy]
Wha* sees nae satire, wit, combin'd [Who]
In Janet Reid.

'Tis true, she's no ower* nice wi' rhyme — [over]
A harmless fault, but no a crime —
The step 'ridic'lous' and 'sublime'
Is worthless creed —
Nane* tak's the forelock grip o' time [None]
Like Janet Reid.

The bonnie lasses braw an' fair*, [fine]
Wha* visit here for change o' air, [Who]
In whirling phaetons* flee nae mair [carriages]
By glen or mead —
'Shanks' naigie now, they just maun* share,' [must]
Quo' Janet Reid.

Blawlowan, 1846 *R.G.*

Janet Reid must have composed a poem (which has not been found) condemning the toll-bar at the east end of the Old Brig. The Rev. William Robertson writes in the *New Statistical Account of Scotland* that there were seven turnpike gates within 2 miles of Blawlowan. 'Shanks' naigie [pony]' means 'to walk on one's own legs' and this probably comes from another of Janet's poems which has not been found. 'Blawlowan' is the only house left of the old village of Pathfoot which was demolished by Sir Robert Abercromby (1740-1827) laird of Airthrey Castle on the outskirts of Bridge of Allan.

'Blawlowan' was owned by James Bryce who was a 'retired Stirling bookseller' in the national census of 1851. He provided lodgings according to *The Tourist's Companion through Stirling* edited and published by John Forbes of Stirling in 1848. The poet 'R.G.' may have come to take the mineral waters at the Airthrey Well House – and he must have bought some of Janet Reid's broadsides! A suggestion made by J. Malcolm Allan is that 'R.G.' was Robert Gilfillan (1798-1850) a Scots poet who was born in Dunfermline and later lived in Leith. One of Robert Gilfillan's songs entitled 'The Maid of Allan' is included in Charles Roger's (or Rogers') guide *A Week at Bridge of Allan* (1851-59).

Major John Alexander Henderson (1806-1858) commissioned Charles Roger (1825-1890) to write a guide to Bridge of Allan where the Major was developing his Westerton Estate by feuing [leasing] plots of land. It was published in 1851 entitled *A Week at Bridge of Allan comprising an account of the Airthrey Spa and a Series of Six Excursions around this Rising Watering-place*. He writes:

> Every watering place, we presume […] has its characters – a class of persons generally more addicted to indolence than to industry, but who receive a pseudo-distinction from sundry eccentricities […] or clothing in doggerel rhymes, sentiments threadbare as their vestments, but which are calculated to excite good humoured laughter […]. Of the present characters of the place the most conspicuous is the poetess, Janet Reid, one of the best specimens of the class to which she belongs. Janet writes or utters poetry, such as it is, on any subject, with complete facility, on a moment's warning, and being devoid of anything satirical in her nature, universally indulges in eulogistic strains. Her published pieces are numerous, and by the vending of these to visitors, on their way to and from the Well House, she not only has contrived to eke out a livelihood, but to realize a considerable competency to meet the wants of declining days. Most poets, in whatever state they may have begun life, generally die poor; Janet promises to prove an exception; she may probably leave the world, through the good-natured liberality of the visitors at Bridge of Allan, comparatively rich.
>
> *Charles Roger*

Janet Reid must have remonstrated with Charles Roger about his comment on her riches for in the 2nd edition of *A Week at Bridge of Allan* published in May 1853 he curtails his comments to:

> Her printed pieces are numerous and by the vending of these to the visitors at the Well House she has contrived to eke out a decent livelihood.

This revised description of Janet is repeated in the 3rd edition July 1853 of *A Week at Bridge of Allan.* By this time Charles Roger had come to live in Bridge of Allan to promote his guide. He had been licensed to preach in 1846 by the Presbytery of St Andrews, Fife, of the Established Church of Scotland but he had no secure living.

A Week at Bridge of Allan continued to be published annually with this description of Janet Reid – but in the 9th edition 1859, Charles Rogers ('Rogers' not 'Roger' after he allowed the banns for his marriage on 8 December 1854 to be called at New Logie Kirk, Bridge of Allan, with his name misspelt 'Rogers') writes:

> In the former editions of this work we noticed two persons, Janet Reid and singing Johnnie ['a regular attendant at the morning rendezvous at the Well House'], as the characters of the place. These have both been removed from the scene without leaving any successors. Some of Janet's doggerel verses are still circulated for the amusement of visitors.
>
> *Charles Rogers*

For Janet Reid and 'singing Johnnie' had both died.

The second entry for 'Reid, Janet' in *The Stirling Observer Index: People 1836-1856* (1988) is Janet's obituary which was printed on the 31 August 1854. This obituary is anonymous but it was probably written by Charles Roger judging from its wordiness and by the last sentence which is almost apologetic:

> THE BRIDGE OF ALLAN POETESS
>
> Janet Reid, the poetess of Bridge of Allan, is no more. She had long been in an ailing state, yet she wore well, and, a few weeks ago, died of old age. We know but little of her history before she came to this district, some 12 or 15 years ago. She belonged to the parish of Carnock, in Fife, and it was a benevolent feeling

which first prompted her to attempt stringing verses together. The beadle of the parish had done something to excite Janet's sympathies, and as he was a poor man, and had to go some distance (no doubt sometimes in coarse and indifferent weather) to ring the bell, she thought it would be well if he had a great-coat to keep his old body comfortable, and she resolved to raise one for him by subscription. In this, however, she failed, but resolving not to be foiled in her endeavours, she betook herself to publication, and generously devoted the proceeds to this humane object, and the bellman's coat was at length purchased in Stirling, and sent to him. Janet knew mankind too well to commit the efforts of her genius to the mere publishing community; with laudable industry, after her effusions had been committed to paper by some fair amanuensis, for as she said herself –

> The pen, that valuable thing, I ne'er was learnt to use

she had them printed, in the first instance, on single slips, with a border round them, and then, with her stock in trade, set off through the country disposing of them upon easy terms, at one penny each, though some good-natured persons would give her 6d [old pence] and a 'comfortable cup of tea' to the bargain. In this simple but efficient mode of publication, Janet continued for a number of years, when the ambitious idea struck her of having selections from her 'WORKS', which had now become numerous, separately published in the gorgeous style of a sixpenny volume. We know not what number, if any, of this 'Adition' [sic] of her works remain; but she never again had recourse to the same mode of publication, though she still continued to write, or rather to dictate, up to a period within a little of her death. Janet's style of composition is beyond all criticism. The iambics, dactyles, spondees and other prosodial lumber, with which all our inferior poets from Milton downwards have used to help themselves and their readers, were totally disregarded by Janet, as unworthy of her notice. With her, the notion of compressing the idea within the line never had a place. The line must be extended to hold the idea, however numerous its feet might be. Sometimes a broad octavo page would not contain a line, while again a fourth of the space was quite sufficient.

> The great cause of Janet's popularity consisted in a good-natured easy and *gash* [freely-spoken] garrulity, quite free from scandal, while tinged with a religious and benevolent feeling, which sat easily upon her, and which never assumed an air of bigotry or sham. She was a calm, steady, and, generally speaking, a cheerful body, and her end was in keeping with the even tenour of her way. She was well seen to at last, and enjoyed as much kindly attention as her circumstances admitted. Her closing days, thanks to a few considerate ladies, were surrounded with every comfort she could enjoy; an attentive nurse was provided her; and she passed away in peace. Janet's poetry was exempt from criticism, but she produced something better than good poetry, namely, an inoffensive life. The little money she had saved passed into the hands of her relatives.
>
> [*Charles Roger*]

The reference to a 'comfortable cup of tea' is to Janet Reid's popular poem *On a Comfortable Cup of Tea* which was reprinted at least 32 times mostly headed as an 'Edition'. The quotation given on a separate line probably comes from a slightly different printing of Janet's poem *On Edinburgh City* to the one found. This suggests that Charles Roger too had bought broadsides from Janet Reid!

Bridge of Allan reproduced from 'A Week at Bridge of Allan' (1853) by Charles Roger.

Janet's broadsides can usually be dated by judicious conjecture and by assuming that there are rational explanations for differences and that these are applied consistently though some changes were made at the whim of the printers. Sometimes Janet Reid quotes a date in her poems or she mentions an event that can be dated – evidence of the date of composition of the poem but not of the printing of the broadside for she had some poems reprinted over many years. However, her poems about the New Year would have been printed for only a short time. A few broadsides have the date of printing put on them by the printer. Janet's poems were reset each time they were printed and each printer used a different typeface and different printers' flowers which are often re-arranged. Janet also changes her home or makes changes to the words in her poems or even changes the title – so each printing is different.

She stuck with the printers that she got to know. In Edinburgh she used 'Macdonald' in Carrubbers' Close – a family of printers including a Mrs Macdonald according to the *Scottish Book Trade Index* (an online resource of the National Library of Scotland). In Glasgow she used Hugh Baird at first and then from 1843 she used William Gilchrist. In Paisley she used John Neilson or Thomas Graham who were partners working separately within the same workshop. When living in Bridge of Allan she used the Stirling Observer Office in Stirling. Six of her broadsides have no printer's imprint but three of them can be deduced as printed by Macdonald from the use of the same typeface and the same printers' flowers.

Janet had about ten poems printed as broadsides in one batch which were probably as many as she could carry around. She went to her printer once a month probably with one new poem and nine older ones. William Gilchrist in Glasgow printed *On a Comfortable Cup of Tea* dated March 1842 and printed *On Glasgow's Bonny City* and *Against Sabbath Breakers* both dated April 1842. Two clusters of ten broadsides and one cluster of nine found in three different sources (each cluster almost certainly printed in the same batch) suggest that some people bought one copy of each of the poems that she carried with her as a 'souvenir' of their stay in Bridge of Allan. The date of printing of all the broadsides in a batch can be established by deducing the date of printing of one broadside.

The most popular of Janet's poems were reprinted for many years and by 1842 she was identifying them as a new 'Edition' which was really the number of times the poem had been printed. Broadsides of the 15th 'Edition' of her poem *On Children Going to Church*; of the 7th and 8th 'Editions' of *On Glasgow's Bonny City*; of the 11th, 13th and 17th 'Editions' of *On Humility*; and of the 24th, 26th and 32nd 'Editions' of *On a Comfortable Cup of Tea* have been found. Two printings of *On a Comfortable Cup of Tea* made in 1840 do not have an 'Edition' number which means that Janet began counting in retrospect in 1841. Janet did not number the 'Editions' of other popular poems such as *The Queen's Farewell* which was reprinted many times – so numbering the 'Edition' of some poems was probably her little ploy to encourage even more sales.

Charles Roger makes a poor pun of this in Janet Reid's obituary by referring to the 'Adition' to her works published in 'the gorgeous style of a sixpenny volume'. A copy of this little 'chapbook' (a cheap booklet printed on one leaf of paper that was folded and sold by chapmen or pedlars) entitled *Poems on Various Subjects* by Janet Reid of Bridge of Allan printed in the Stirling Observer Office in 1846 was discovered in the University of Glasgow Library. This chapbook is about half the size of her broadsides and it includes 34 of her poems of which 13 have not been found as broadsides – though they would have been printed as broadsides first. The title of her chapbook may seem to be an uninspired one but this was the conventional title for books of poems at this time. The catalogue of the National Library of Scotland lists about 35 books entitled *Poems on Various Subjects* by different authors published between 1777 (Janet's birth) and 1846 – though not this one!

Sixty different poems composed by Janet Reid have been found – 47 as broadsides and another 13 in her chapbook. How many poems did she compose? Well, she began composing in 1836 and she continued into 1853 which is 16 years. It is evident that in 1842 she had her poems printed at the rate of at least one new poem a month. So, even allowing for a lower rate in her early and her later years, she must have composed well over 100 poems. Probably only half of the poems that she composed have been discovered.

Seventy-one broadsides of Janet Reid's poems have been found including duplicate copies of the same printing of three of them. These 71 broadsides comprise a single broadside of 33 poems; two broadsides of eight poems; three broadsides of *On the Gallant Sailors*, *The Queen's Farewell* and *On Glasgow, Bonny Town* or *On Glasgow's Bonny City* (the same poem with a change in title); four broadsides of *On Humility* and *On the Spring*; and five broadsides of *On a Comfortable Cup of Tea*. The number surviving is probably another indication of the relative popularity of her poems.

All Janet's broadsides have a decorative border of printers' flowers which often give them a touch of elegance. Most of the 1,800 broadsides reproduced online under *The Word on the Street* on the website of the National Library of Scotland are either of plain text or have a woodcut picture at their head; only about one in sixty have a decorative border of printers' flowers. So Janet must have specially requested her printers to use them – though the printers would have charged her extra as they did for the use of a woodcut picture.

Newspapers in the early 1800s were dull, expensive and taxed until 1855. Broadsides were the popular reading matter. They could be written in verse, prose or song and they could be religious, political, romantic, bawdy, funny or tragic. Some of them were passed down and almost all were composed anonymously. Henry Mayhew (1812-1887) writes in *London Labour and the London Poor* (1851) that broadsides were bought from the printers by different kinds of pedlars that were named from the way they sold their wares: 'flying stationers', 'standing patterers', 'running patterers', 'long-song sellers', 'wall-song sellers', 'pinners-up', or 'ballad sellers'. No doubt Janet would have 'chaunted' her wares like they did.

Janet Reid's earnings would have fluctuated throughout the year but to earn a living-wage she had to keep on selling her broadsides in all weathers all the year round. How many broadsides did Janet have printed during those 16 years? If Janet went to her printer once a month and had 144 copies (a gross) of ten different poems printed each time, she would have sold about 276,000 copies over those 16 years. This means that only one copy of her broadsides has survived for every 4,000 copies sold.

To put this into context, Leslie Shepard in *The History of Street Literature* (1973) writes that James Catnach of London printed 250,000 copies of a single broadside about a murder in 1824; and Michael J. McCormack describes in *The Stirling Tract Enterprise and the Drummonds* (1984) how Peter Drummond of Stirling printed 260,000 copies of his first religious tract *The Sabbath* in 1848. Leslie Shepard quotes a price of one shilling a gross as the price for quarter-sheet broadsides – and Janet's are half this size. So, if she sold her broadsides at a halfpenny or a penny each, she would have had an income after paying her printer of about £50 a year or double the earnings of a skilled workman by selling about 1,720 broadsides a month or 70 a day (though not on the Sabbath).

Peter Forbes' bookplate is mounted on the endpaper of his album with a crest and a motto: '*Nec Timide Nec Temere*' (Neither Timidly nor Rashly) which is ascribed to Sir William Forbes (1739-1836) of Monymusk and New Pitsligo in Aberdeenshire. Peter Forbes probably acquired these broadsides in the 1870s judging from his album which is not hand-marbled but printed. Two of Sir William Forbes' descendants were contemporary with Peter Forbes: Sir William's grandson James David Forbes (1809-1865) and James' second son George Forbes (1849-1936) both eminent scholars. The crest was probably appropriated by an unrelated Peter Forbes.

Nine of the broadsides in Peter Forbes' album were found to be printed in the same batch in 1843. J. Malcolm Allan of Bridge of Allan spotted eleven of Janet's broadsides listed in the Short-Title Catalogue of the British Library. Ten of these were found to be printed in the same batch in 1846. Larry Hutchison (a dealer in Scottish and Antiquarian Books in Dunfermline) told me about the eleven broadsides by Janet Reid kept in Dunfermline Carnegie Library. These were given by Erskine Beveridge (1853-1920) with his book collection on Dunfermline and the West of Fife. Ten of these were found to be printed in the same batch in late 1842. All three batches were printed in the Stirling Observer Office.

Further inquiries found nine broadsides by Janet Reid in the Mitchell Library, Glasgow; two more in an album in the British Library; and two in the Scottish National Library one of which was put online under *The Word on the Street*. Another broadside in the Wellcome Library, London, and Janet's chapbook *Poems on Various Subjects* (1846) in Glasgow University Library were found through COPAC, an online merged catalogue of National and Academic libraries.

In *A Bibliography of Works Relating to Dunfermline and the West of Fife* (1901), Erskine Beveridge lists eighteen poems by Janet Reid: the eleven broadsides in his possession plus seven titles given 'on outside authority' six of these being new poems among the eleven by Janet Reid in the British Museum (now in the British Library) and another entitled *On Peace in Every Church* which has not been found. He then adds: 'And many more' and remarks of her:

> Born at Saline, 1777; resident at Carnock 1825-1840 or later; quite a character in her way – that of composing doggerel rhymes upon any (or every) subject. These she had printed in broadside form, commencing about 1836 and sold them from door to door. Latterly she removed to Bridge of Allan where she died. It is said that Jenny Reid was unable to write but her neighbours did this for her.

An anonymous note dated 31 July 1894 is kept with Janet Reid's broadsides in Dunfermline Carnegie Library. This note is written on a folded leaf of paper which once enclosed a broadside – for there are four strips of old postage-stamp margin placed diagonally inside it evidently put there to hold a broadside by its four corners. This note was almost certainly sent with the broadside of the poem *On the Honourable Manufacturers of Dunfermline* when it was given to Erskine Beveridge presumably as a token of goodwill because this poem mentions his father 'Mr Beveridge' who was another Erskine Beveridge (1803-1864). He was the owner of Erskine Beveridge & Company the weavers of damask-linen employing 800 workers in Dunfermline. Erskine Beveridge, Junior, succeeded his father as the owner when he was 11 years old and his father died.

The anonymous writer's note and his handwriting give the impression of him being elderly and not too astute – for he says of Janet Reid (in the second part of this note) that: 'The following account was probably written by herself ', when the account itself says that she could not write! The first part of this anonymous note which was sent to Erskine Beveridge, Junior, is a greeting:

> *Success I wish to Mr Beveridge. Honour to the Three Erskines.*
> *A good three fold cord. May the manhood entered on today*
> *stretch far into the coming years; and both the later Erskines*
> *emulate the honours of their sires.* *July 31st 1894*

The 'Three Erskines' were Erskine Beveridge, Junior, and his two surviving sons: John born on 2 August 1874 and David born on 4 November 1886. 'A good threefold cord' alludes to the saying in the Bible: 'A three-fold cord is not quickly broken'. The writer of this note may not have known Erskine Beveridge except by repute – nor may the writer of the note have been known to Erskine Beveridge, Junior, at all – for neither of his two sons were named 'Erskine' and John became aged 20 at this time, not 21. The note which was sent to Erskine Beveridge, Junior, enclosing the broadside of *On the Honourable Manufacturers of Dunfermline* has a second part which is a description of Janet Reid:

> *Janet Reid was born near Carnock in the West Neuk of Fife in 1777. The following acct. was probably written by herself on 19th Sep 1840. Janet Reid's first beginning of Poetry was about 4 years since, when some of her neighbours were wishing to give a coat to the Bell-man. A young man had written the subscription Paper; & after he had gotten subscriptions the young man took away the Paper again; & the old man did not get his coat. Janet was angry at this & made a Copy of verses on him, & recited it to*

the neighbours in revenge. They approved of it; and urged her to do more. And once Captain Wemyss, who the Carnock folk wanted to be made a Parliament man, and on whom she had made a bonnie Poem sent her a Pound. This encouraged her to go on, although she thought shame of it at first. She cannot write; but her neighbours write her verses for her.

Astonishingly, this description of Janet Reid is the story dated 19 September 1840 written (in a different hand) by the purchaser on the broadside of *On the Mid-Mill* which was found in Peter Forbes' album! So it was Peter Forbes who wrote the note and it was he who sent the broadside to Erskine Beveridge in 1894. There are marks in the album showing that the last broadside has been removed.

Why didn't Peter Forbes tell Erskine Beveridge his name and the titles of his other broadsides by Janet Reid? Erskine Beveridge would then have listed them in his *A Bibliography of Works Relating to Dunfermline and the West of Fife* (1901). Perhaps Peter Forbes' wanted to guard his 'treasure' and his silence was a collector's secretiveness. Erskine Beveridge probably never discovered who wrote the anonymous note in 1894 and who gave him the broadside of *On the Honourable Manufacturers of Dunfermline*.

The Old Brig o' Allan drawn about 1845 looking upriver.

Charles Dickens (1812-1870) and his wife Catharine Hogarth (born in Edinburgh) visited Scotland during June 1841 when he was granted the Freedom of the City of Edinburgh. They left Edinburgh on 4 July 1841 to make a tour of the Scottish Highlands passing through Bridge of Allan without stopping. If Charles Dickens had halted at the Airthrey Well, Janet Reid might have been the inspiration for a deservedly Dickensian character in *Barnaby Rudge* (1841) instalments of which he wrote on this visit to Scotland!

In *The Fife Herald* printed in Cupar in the East Neuk of Fife on 21 September 1854 under the sub-heading 'Compendium' there is a 'tall story' by Charles Dickens and a note about Janet Reid:

> Janet Reid, the well-known Bridge of Allan
> poetess who for many years wandered through
> the country selling her poems, is dead.

In the *Aberdeen Journal and General Advertiser for the North of Scotland* on 13 September 1854 the first item at the head of the third column of 'Local Intelligence' describes the journey of Queen Victoria and Prince Albert by rail to Aberdeen to stay at Balmoral Castle on Deeside, Aberdeenshire. Beneath this is a brief note:

> Janet Reid, the Bridge of Allan poetess, who
> has wandered through the country selling her
> rhymes for many years, has died of old age.

The Old Parish Registers in Scotland record births or baptisms and marriages before 1855; and the 'lair' [grave] books record burials but there is no record of Janet Reid's burial in 1854 in the County Archives of Stirling nor in those of Fife. Her gravestone is not in the Old Kirkyard at Logie Old Kirk, nor in the churchyard at New Logie Kirk, nor in the churchyard at Lecropt Kirk, nor in the Old Kirkyard in Saline nor in the Old Kirkyard in Carnock; an inscription is not included in *East Stirlingshire Monumental Inscriptions Pre-1855* (1997) nor in *Fifeshire Monumental Inscriptions (Pre-1855): The Western Parishes* (2001) both compiled by John Fowler Mitchell and Sheila Mitchell. Janet is probably buried in an unmarked grave in the churchyard at New Logie Kirk (opened in 1809 and enlarged in 1901), the parish church of the parish in which she last resided, 2 miles east of Bridge of Allan.

Charles Rogers in *Monuments and Monumental Inscriptions in Scotland* (1871-72) quotes an epitaph that was once to be found in Torryburn churchyard 2 miles south of Carnock:

> In this churchyard lies Eppie Coutts,
> Either here or hereabouts;
> But whaur* it is there's nane* can tell, [where, none]
> Till Eppie rise and tell hersel*. [herself]

And so it is for Janet Reid: her poems are her memorial. She overdid her religious exhortations, she was repetitive, and her poems are not amusing – not even unintentionally like those of William McGonagall (1825-1902) who sold his 'poetic gems' as broadsides thirty years later on the streets of Dundee. Like him, Janet composed with an eye to sales and her eulogistic verse was composed to fulfil her constant need for new poems to attract new buyers.

Janet Reid had more affinity with Janet Hamilton (1795-1873) 'the Langloan poetess' of Lanarkshire who also never went to school. Her mother taught her to read from the Bible and she only learnt to write in single letters. She began composing poems in Scots and in English in her 50s, she became blind at 60 and she dictated her poems to her son. They were first published in the 1860s and are moving (very different to Janet Reid's). Janet Hamilton once said: 'You might as well ask the laverock [lark] how it can sing as ask me how I can write according to the rules of grammarians'.

Every written or printed reference that I have found to Janet Reid is quoted here. Janet Reid, Jenny Reid, old Janet Reid or 'poem Jenny' was honest, principled and hard-working as well as canny. Janet helped free a woman wrongly accused of killing a child; she gave the profit from selling the broadsides of one poem to an injured workman's family; she urged the rich to help the poor; she campaigned against cruelty to horses; and she urged freedom for young ladies to choose a young man. Janet is memorable – even if her verse is not. She fended for herself – she never married though it is evident from her poems that she would have liked to have a husband. She was outspoken in her 'unpolished' poems and they can be read for their historical interest – and for the pleasure they give.

ON A COMFORTABLE CUP OF TEA.

I WONDER how people in drunkenness can delight,
For very often drunkenness ends in spite.
A comfortable cup of tea will neither harm you nor me.
Them that only take a cup of tea,
To their neighbours they'll have another to gi'e.
Round the tea-table there is contentment and peace,
They choose a respectable man to say a grace.
The third commandment at the tea-table is seldom broke,
With one another they often pass a harmless joke.
But with the drunkard it is not often so,
God's law they often break, and prove one another's foe.
If poor people would look forward to grey hairs and clothing
thin,
They would hang the little gill-stoup on a pin,
And slip awa' hame with their drunken groat,
And think on the time they may need a new coat.
To beggary with drink many a one does come,
For in my lifetime I have seen some.
Thomas Boston speaks of an inn by the way,
But people should not very long there stay.
I wish all drunken people the 5th of Galatians to read,
And with sober people begin to take up their head—
All them that do love a cup of tea;
It is not like whisky, and that you'll see:
These are the proper company for you and me.
Tea parties meet in friendship and end in peace,
To young nor old they'll never bring disgrace.
All drunkards, I hope, will take an advice from me,
Give over drinking whisky, and take a good cup of tea.
I hope good people God's goodness will not forget,
While round the tea-table they do sit.

JANET REID, CARNOCK.

J. Neilson, Printer, Paisley.

Peter Forbes' album. *Printed by John Neilson, Paisley, 1840.*
[*See the poem on page 42*]

JANET REID'S 'UNPOLISHED' POEMS

ON THE HONOURABLE MANUFACTURERS OF DUNFERMLINE.

Success I wish to Mr Dewar,
For he was always kind unto the poor ;
Success I wish to Mr Cooper,
He gave the weavers silver and copper ;
Success I wish to Mr Hunt,
I hope him nor his will never want ;
Success to Messrs Walker, Fergie, and Bryce,
To hold on the weavers' side they are very wise ;
Success I wish to Mr Beveridge,
For he gave the weavers work when they were ike to perish ;
Success to all the rest I do not know,
I hope none of them will ever prove the weavers' foe ;
But as for the weavers' enemies,
They deserve a proper tease ;
They have surely never read the 13th chapter of St. Luke,
Or they would have seen how the rich man got his rebuke.
I wonder how the rich the poor can so despise,
For in hell the rich man lifted up his eyes,
Against the weavers they should not be so severe,
Before Christ's judgement-seat they must all appear ;
They have surely never read Christ's sermon on the mount,
Or about the weavers' wages they would never chunt ;
I wish them to read the ninety-fourth psalm,
And to the honourable weavers to be always calm ;
Unto the weavers' enemies here I have no name,
But cheipicks and dandylerie they surely are to blame.

JANET REID, *Carnock.*

Dunfermline Carnegie Library. [*No printer's imprint – possibly printed in Edinburgh, 1840*]

ON THE HONOURABLE MANUFACTURERS OF DUNFERMLINE

Success I wish to Mr Dewar,
For he was always kind unto the poor;
Success I wish to Mr Cooper,
He gave the weavers silver and copper;
Success I wish to Mr Hunt,
I hope him nor his will never want;
Success to Messrs Walker, Fergie and Bryce,
To hold on the weavers' side they are very wise;
Success I wish to Mr Beveridge,
For he gave the weavers work when they were ike*
to perish; [like]
Success to all the rest I do not know,
I hope none of them will ever prove the weavers' foe;
But as for the weavers' enemies,
They deserve a proper tease*; [vexation]
They have surely never read the thirteenth chapter of
St Luke,
Or they would have seen how the rich man got his
rebuke.
I wonder how the rich the poor can so despise,
For in hell the rich man lifted up his eyes;
Against the weavers they should not be so severe,
Before Christ's judgement-seat they must all appear;
They have surely never read Christ's Sermon on the
Mount,
Or about the weavers' wages they would never chunt*, [grumble]
I wish them to read the ninety-fourth Psalm,
And to the honourable weavers to be always calm;
Unto the weavers' enemies here I have no name,
But cheipicks* and dandylerie* they surely are to
blame. [cheap stuff ?, finery?]

Janet Reid, 1837.

JANET REID'S broadsides were printed in Dunfermline before 1840 though no copies have been found. Erskine Beveridge, Junior, did not recognize *On the Honourable Manufacturers of Dunfermline* as having been printed in Dunfermline in his bibliography. Christopher Neale of Dunfermline Carnegie Library compared early printed material in the Library (largely given by Erskine Beveridge, Junior) with the broadsides of *On the Honourable Manufacturers of Dunfermline* and *On the Year 1841* and the earliest copy found of *On the Gallant Sailors* (all of them without a printer's imprint) and concluded that none of them were printed in Dunfermline.

Of the three printers in Dunfermline at this time, John Miller & Son (1835-1863) is probably the most likely to have printed Janet Reid's broadsides. The story of James Miller of Haddington, George Miller of Dunbar and John Miller of Dunfermline is told in *The Millers of Haddington, Dunbar and Dunfermline: a record of Scottish bookselling* (1914) by W.J. Couper. John Miller (1780-1852) was born in Dunfermline but his mother died in childbirth and his father died when he was aged 9. He was brought up by his elder half-brothers, James Miller and George Miller, who were printers and booksellers. John lived with and was apprenticed to George Miller in Dunbar and worked for him as a journeyman printer.

In 1805 John Miller set up on his own in Dunfermline in the south-west corner of Abbey Park Place (where there is a memorial plaque to him) with the money left him by his father which had been preserved by his half-brothers. George Miller bought him a large Dutch printing press as a parting gift. John married Helen Laing in 1806, moved to Bridge Street, Dunfermline, in 1807 and took his 24-year old son, John Laing Miller, into partnership in 1835.

John Miller, hitherto a seceder within the Presbyterian Church of Scotland, became a Baptist and John Laing Miller married Jane Moncrieff, the daughter of the Baptist pastor of Dunfermline, in 1841 by whom he had 'numerous' children (who coloured his chapbooks). John Laing Miller was a Baptist Sabbath School superintendent and he played the 'seraphim', a precursor of the harmonium, which he introduced into Baptist Sunday services at a time when the Scottish Presbyterian church forbade the singing of hymns or the use of musical instruments in church services.

ON THE SPRING

Now it is com'd the months of the Spring,
And the small birds on many a tree doth sing.
The seed has now got a dry bed;
I hope at harvest-time we'll all be glad.
One person may plant and another may water,
But man can do no more but the seed to scatter.
In every season, day and hour, we may see God's power,
And his wonders even in the smallest flower.
Youth is like unto a flower that grows in summer,
The beauties and pleasures of it is very soon gone over.
Our life-time is like unto a year or a day;
But with man and woman Time is flying fast away.
Young ones is like the months of March and April,
At that time of life they're easy to beguile.
Youths are like the months of May and June,
But these months, like all others, will soon run done.
Mid-age is like unto September and October,
In all seasons of our life we should be sober.
The short days of December comes last of all,
And the leaves from every tree at that time does fall.
In righteousness we should all take delight,
That we may be found at last among the white*. [chosen]
We should often think on Christ's sufferings in the Garden and
on the Tree*, [Cross]
How he suffered for sinners such as you and me.
Some people would our blessed Saviour fain* deny, [willingly]
But death and judgment in a short time will us try.
We should all mind Christ's golden rule,
And unto one another we should never be cruel.
Before Christ's judgment-seat we must all appear,
For our actions, good or bad, we have done here.
With many a one at this day it is the Spring,
But with some others their year is also in decline.
Sure people will not be always young,
Some good by everyone in their day should be done.

Janet Reid, 1837. [See one of the four broadsides on page 138]

ON 25 January 1862 (eight years after the death of Janet Reid) *The Saturday Press*, a Dunfermline local newspaper, printed a report headed 'Handsel Monday in London' (the first Monday of the New Year when gifts were given in Scotland) mentioning Janet and her poem *Dunfermline Notabilities or The Light of Other Days* (probably composed in 1837) which has not been found:

> On the evening of Monday, January 13 [1862], upwards of twenty gentlemen – natives and old residents of Dunfermline – met to celebrate the festival of Auld Handsel Monday in the City of London. The supper, which was provided at the 'Scotch Stores', Road Lane, was in strict keeping with the occasion; sheep's head and haggis forming two of the dishes. […] The cloth being removed, the Chairman, in stating the object of the meeting, said that it had its origin in a chance meeting of six or seven Dunfermline men, who agreed to meet on the night of Auld Handsel Monday: 'to eat a piece of roast beef with a Scotch haggis, drink to absent friends, and sing "Auld Langsyne" together'. This was the first meeting of the kind, but he hoped it would not be the last. The Chairman then gave in succession the usual loyal and patriotic toasts. […] He then proposed the toast of the evening: 'Dunfermline and its Association', dwelling on the pleasures of meeting with fellow-townsmen in a strange land, and of the thoughts of auld langsyne to which such meetings gave rise; of the time when they sported among the ruins of auld grey Dunfermline […] and hummed amid their play – 'The King sits in Dunfermline toon, drinking the bluid red wyne' [from the 18th-century ballad *Sir Patrick Spens*, when Dunfermline was the seat of Scottish Kings] […] and the songs of their local poets [...].
>
> He concluded by reciting extracts from a poem, composed by the late Janet Reid, a well-known 'character', entitled *Dunfermline Notabilities or The Light of Other Days*, the many numerous allusions of which kept the company in a continual roar of laughter. […] The proceedings were throughout of a most interesting and thrilling nature, and the company broke up at an early hour next morning, all concurring in the hope expressed by the Chairman in his opening speech, that this might not be the last occasion on which the Dunfermline folks in London should meet together to celebrate their 'Auld Monday'.

LAMENT FOR A BELOVED MINISTER

This has brought on Saline people a sore vexation,
For in their heart to their minister there was a near relation;
It's always the genuine feeling of the heart
That makes any people for to smart.
The Psalmist, David, he did say –
Ere I afflicted was, I went astray.
Our blessed Saviour, when on earth, did also say –
Believers all take up your cross and come away.
At this present time Saline's people's loss
To them, both rich and poor, has been a sore cross.
I hope it will lead old and young to a throne of grace,
To pray that they may meet him in a better place.
Their beloved minister for them will pray
That they may stand on Christ's right hand at the last day.
I hope their beloved minister and them will meet
Where tears will never run down any cheek.
Because his dwelling is so far from their own place,
That makes the tears run down many a face.
There's but a meeting here and then to part again.
It's but a few short years any of us will on earth remain.
We should all learn contented to be,
Many is the alteration every year we see.
We should always see God's hand in everything,
For he brings it about in his own way and time.
We should always set our hearts beyond the grave,
Where, through Christ's sufferings, pleasures evermore we'll have.
All in this world is vanity; it's all a vain show;
We should never set our hearts on anything here below.
If Kirkintilloch were within the sight of Carnock steeple,
In Saline there would be happy people.
I hope Saline people will always live in peace,
And every day they live will grow in grace.

Janet Reid, 1837.

ON A COMFORTABLE CUP OF TEA

I wonder how people in drunkenness can delight,
For often drunkenness ends in spite.
A comfortable cup of tea will neither harm you nor me.
Them that only take a cup of tea,
To their neighbours they'll have another to gi'e*. [give]
Round the tea-table there is contentment and peace,
They choose a respectable man to say a grace.
The third commandment at the tea-table is seldom broke,
With one another they often pass a harmless joke.
But with the drunkard it is not often so,
God's law they often break, and prove one another's foe.
If poor people would look forward to grey hairs and clothing thin,
They would hang the little gill-stoup* on a pin, [quarter-pint pot]
And slip awa' hame with their drunken groat*, [four-penny coin]
And think on the time they may need a new coat.
If working people would save threepence a week,
They would sometimes have need for it when they were sick.
Though it is but a halfpenny a day,
Perhaps they would see need for it when once their hairs grow grey.
To beggary with drink many a one does come,
For in my lifetime I have seen some.
Thomas Boston speaks of an inn by the way,
But people should not very long there stay.
I wish all drunken people the fifth of Galatians to read,
And with sober people begin to take up their head –
All them that do love a good cup of tea,
It is not like whisky, and that you'll see –
These are the proper company for you and me.
Tea parties meet in friendship and end in peace,
To young or old they'll never bring disgrace.
All drunkards, I hope, will take an advice from me –
Give over drinking whisky, and take a good cup of tea.
I hope good people God's council will not forget,
While round the tea-table they do sit.

Janet Reid, 1838. [See one of the five broadsides on page 33]

ON CHILDREN GOING TO CHURCH

As soon as children have wit still to sit,
Unto the church they should always be put;
For a time they do little good – they do as little ill,
As soon as they have wisdom for to sit still.
Perhaps some people's children may not be very braw*, [admirable]
But, for all this, in their youth Death may give them a ca'*. [call]
When we go past our neighbours' graves on every side,
Young and old may see the very little need of pride.
It is better to go to God's house bareheaded and unshod,
Than to break the Sabbath with wicked children on the road.
Mind what King Solomon, the preacher, did say –
Train up your children always in the way.
When I was a little child I was sent to a tent*, [field-pulpit]
Many other children along with me there went.
Upon the green I was not very braw,
But I heard the sermon as well as the grandest of them a'*. [all]
Unto this day the text I can you tell –
Isaiah thirty-five verse ten, there you'll see it yoursel'.
Set before your children always a good example,
If they live till they're old they'll likely keep the sample.
None would wish to see their children at Christ's left hand,
When once in judgment we must all stand.
Be sure before little children to read and pray;
I hope you will lead young ones in the right way.
This was done by one who never was at school,
On the Sabbath day never let your children act the fool.
As parents for their children's bodies do prepare,
I hope for their souls they will take great care.

Janet Reid, 1838.

THE population of Scotland was 2,620,184 in the 1841 national census. These are the places that Janet Reid visited (or may have visited) and the number of their inhabitants as given in the *New Statistical Account of Scotland* (compiled 1834-45):

Glasgow	202,426	(1831 census)
Edinburgh and Leith	163,726	(1841 census)
Paisley	57,880	(1841 census)
Dunfermline	19,778	(1841 census)
Stirling	8,914	(1841 census)
Falkirk	7,445	(1831 census)
Kirkintilloch	5,888	(1831 census)
Kirkcaldy	5,034	(1831 census)
Dunblane	3,367	(1841 census)
Bridge of Allan	200	(1841 census)

The parish of Saline had a population of 1,057 in the 1841 census of which about 400 lived in the village. The Rev. William Forfar (1756-1844), the minister of Saline from 1793 to 1843, reports in *The 'Old' Statistical Account of Scotland* (compiled 1791-99):

> There are no epidemical diseases peculiar to this parish. There are some instances of longevity, as in other places. Several have lived above 80; some above 90; one or two above 100.

The parish of Carnock had a population of 1,269 in the 1841 census of which about 400 lived in this village. The Rev. Alexander Thomson, minister of Carnock from 1780 to 1793, reports in *The 'Old' Statistical Account of Scotland* (compiled 1791-99):

> The small-pox generally visits the parish once in 3 or 4 years. The four last returns were in 1780, 1783, 1787 and 1789. That of 1787 was by far the most severe when 15 children out of 45 died [...]; and that of 1789 the most favourable when only 3 died out of 63 [. . .]. In 1780 and 1783 the medium of deaths was from 4 to 6 each year, though a great many had that disease.

The Rev. William Robertson, minister of the parish of Logie from 1832 to 1843, writes in the *New Statistical Account of Scotland* (compiled 1834-45) that the population of Lecropt (west of the Allan Water) was 471; and that of Logie (east of the Allan Water) was 1,943 in the 1841 national census.

ON HUMILITY

When people need a new coat or new gown,
On the counter the merchants their goods will put down.
Although the people should wear many a braw* dress, [fine]
We should aye take the Bible for our looking-glass.
We should always keep in mind how clothing did begin –
The best of clothes are only but the badge of sin.
In our braw clothes we should always be sober and meek;
Remember we must soon change them for a winding sheet.
We should never be proud of a braw new coat or gown;
Remembering that Christ of thorns wore a crown.
It is not braw clothes that makes the pride,
For there is many a humble one in their coach do ride.
There is sometimes more pride below a ragged coat,
Than is with many a one that in their coaches do trot.
The Lord unto the humble He grace doth gi'e*, [give]
Whereas the proud afar off only knoweth He.
We have nothing in this world at all to make us proud,
But that our Saviour for our sins came good.
We should always remember what our sins our Saviour cost,
Had it not been our blessed Saviour we should have all been lost.
A gallant young woman in Carnock did die,
'Be humble, be humble,' and called for her Bible, was her last cry.
She was a pretty youth as ever I did see,
But her winding sheet her dress was soon to be.
In the church-yard, when we do see our neighbour's grave,
It teaches us, young and old, soberly to behave.
Although about our Bible we sometimes prove shy,
The death of the righteous we all would wish to die.
We should always be giving one another good advice,
That through Christ's merits we may hope to meet in paradise.
All they who came to Jesus in faith He ne'er did deny,
For He stood still and heard poor blind Bartimeus cry.

Janet Reid, 1838.

ON GIVING WORK TO WORKING FOLK.

There is a worthy Gentleman lives near our place;
Many is the working people that loves to see his face.
In a time of dull trade to work-folk he is well bred,
He employs many a one with both mell and spade;
Many a blessing on him people does often wish,
Because to find work for them he did strongly push.
If working-people work could always find,
They would not surely be left far behind.
When poor people work they cannot get
Sure them and their families solitary must sit.
The mason makes the wa's stand firm and tight,
And after the mason then comes the wright,
And then comes the slater, with his broad slate,
After him the roof looks firm and neat;
The plumber, with his long spouts, comes last of all,
And makes the water run handsomely round the wall;
The plasterer he does not very long remain,
After him the wright he soon comes back again.
Good people, I do not wish you longer to entertain,
Because there is some of my subjects but very mean.
For my uneven lines you will me excuse,
Because the pen, that valuable thing, I never could use.
I wish the worthy Gentleman and all his men
May meet hereafter in heaven again.
I hope they will read the hundred and nineteenth Psalm,
And to one another be always calm.
The 25th chapter of Matthew we should not forget,
And mind out of our earthly dwellings we all must flit.

JANET REID, CARNOCK.

Baird, Printer, 174, Trongate, Glasgow.

Peter Forbes' album. *Printed by Hugh Baird, Glasgow, 1840.*

ON GIVING WORK TO WORKING FOLK

There is a worthy Gentleman lives near our place,
Many is the working people that loves to see his face.
In a time of dull trade to work-folk he is well bred,
He employs many a one with both mell* and spade. [mason's
Many a blessing on him people does often wish, hammer]
Because to find work for them he did strongly push.
If working-people work could always find,
They would not surely be left far behind.
When poor people work they cannot get,
Sure them and their families solitary must sit.
The mason makes the wa's* stand firm and tight, [walls]
And after the mason then comes the wright*; [carpenter]
And then comes the slater, with his broad slate,
After him the roof looks firm and neat;
The plumber, with his long spouts, comes last of all,
And makes the water run handsomely round the wall;
The plasterer he does not very long remain;
After him the wright he soon comes back again.
Good people, I do not wish you longer to entertain,
Because there is some of my subjects but very mean.
For my uneven lines you will me excuse,
Because the pen, that valuable thing, I never could use.
I wish the worthy Gentleman and all his men
May meet hereafter in heaven again.
I hope they will read the hundred and nineteenth Psalm,
And to one another be always calm.
The twenty-fifth chapter of St Matthew we should not forget,
And mind out of our earthly dwellings we must all flit.

Janet Reid, 1839.

ON CRUEL MURDER.

A cruel murder of late did take place—.
Carnock's little village they thought to disgrace;
They surely have very little skill,
That took away poor Bennie, that lives beside the mill.
Perhaps they might have come from Dunfermline town,
That laid this little innocent child down;
Or even they might have taken a turn,
And come all the way from Torryburn.
They had intended for this child a watery grave,
I wish people afterwards themselves may better behave.
The murderer has gotten a screen,
To abuse poor Bennie, I know not what they mean.
Although the murderer from man's eye did fly,
For all this they cannot escape God's all seeing eye.
I wish there may not be another murder in the bush,
But poor Bennie for the murder they did so sorely crush.
When they got poor Bennie locked up in a cell,
The murderer might escape full well.
It was a cruel murder that had been done,
To cut the innocent infant's very tongue.
Some person the infant did both kill and drown,
But Our BENNIE'S Infant has got a braw white gown.
Now we have got back poor Bennie beside the mill,
And pretending people have lost all their skill.
Had it not been another old woman and me,
Poor Bennie and her child would had to die.
Some people think they have surely little sin,
To reproach poor Bennie they did soon begin.
Now we have got poor Bennie out of the cell,
And thanks be to God, who ruleth all things well.
Women have not got a rabbit's nature,
In every month to bring forth a young creature.
I have lived a long time in the west neuk o' Fife,
And I never knew the like of that all my life.
The like was never in Perth, as little in Dundee,
To judge a woman for child-murder, and her infant on her knee.

JANET REID, CARNOCK.

Macdonald, Printer, Carrubbers' Close.

Wellcome Library. *Printed by Macdonald, Edinburgh, 1840.*

ON CRUEL MURDER

A cruel murder of late did take place –
Carnock's little village they thought to disgrace;
They surely have very little skill,
That took away poor Bennie that lives beside the mill.
Perhaps they might have come from Dunfermline town,
That laid this little innocent child down;
Or even they might have taken a turn,
And come all the way from Torryburn.
They had intended for this child a watery grave;
I wish people afterwards themselves may better behave.
The murderer has gotten a screen*, [shelter]
To abuse poor Bennie, I know not what they mean.
Although the murderer from man's eye did fly,
For all this they cannot escape God's all-seeing eye.
I wish there may not be another murder in the bush,
But poor Bennie for the murder they did so sorely crush.
When they got poor Bennie locked up in a cell,
The murderer might escape full well.
It was a cruel murder that has been done,
To cut the innocent infant's very tongue.
Some person the infant did both kill and drown,
But Our Bennie's Infant has got a braw white gown.
Now we have got back poor Bennie beside the mill,
And pretending people have lost all their skill.
Had it not been another old woman and me,
Poor Bennie and her child would had to die.
Some people think they have surely little sin,
To reproach poor Bennie they did soon begin.
Now we have got poor Bennie out of the cell,
And thanks be to God, who ruleth all things well.
Women have not got a rabbit's nature,
In every month to bring forth a young creature.
I have lived a long time in the West Neuk* o' Fife, [Corner]
And I never knew the like of that all my life.
The like was never in Perth, as little in Dundee,
To judge a woman for child-murder, and her infant on her knee.

Janet Reid, 1839.

WHEN Janet Reid began to think about travelling further afield to sell her broadsides it would be natural for her to think of the four major destinations of the stage-coaches that passed close to Carnock or through Dunfermline.

Travellers going east or west from Carnock could take the stage-coach *Aurora* that ran daily between Kirkcaldy in the East Neuk [Corner] of Fife via Dunfermline, Cairneyhill (2 miles south of Carnock), Stirling (the most seaward bridge over the River Forth at this time), Falkirk (where a traveller could change to a passenger-boat at Lock 16 on the Forth and Clyde Canal), Kirkintilloch (also on the Forth and Clyde Canal) and Glasgow.

Travellers going north or south from Carnock could take the stage-coach *Antiquary* that ran daily between Perth via Dunfermline and the Queensferry Passage across the Firth of Forth and Edinburgh. From 1838 to 1863 the ferryboat was the *William Adam* which was a small iron paddle-steamer that towed several sailing ships – the Queensferry crossing was particularly difficult for sailing ships because of the strength of the tidal current.

Janet Reid did go to Edinburgh and she did go to Glasgow. Perth is on the River Tay and had overseas trade but Kirkcaldy (known as the 'Lang Toon') was in her home county of Fife and it had a busy harbour with a thriving overseas trade in imports and exports. There were sailors and there would have been 'carpenters' (boat-builders) in Kirkcaldy, so there were potential buyers for her poem *On the Gallant Sailors* which she probably composed there. There were no sailors in Carnock or Dunfermline though there were harbours at Limekilns and at Charlestown both 3 miles south-west of Dunfermline but these were for shipping coal and lime. So probably Janet decided to visit Kirkcaldy in 1839 to see how she would fare at selling her broadsides away from Dunfermline.

Afterwards, Janet returned to Carnock bidding 'adieu'. 'Adieu' is used in broadside ballads when going on a long journey. In Kirkcaldy the 'The Kirkcaldy Whale Fishing Company' owned sixteen whaling ships that sailed to the North Atlantic off Greenland over the period from 1816 to 1866. That could be why Janet mentions 'Jonah out of the fish' (Jonah who was swallowed by the whale in the Bible) in *On the Gallant Sailors*!

ON THE GALLANT SAILORS

The Carpenters make the ships both firm and stout,
And to the seas the Sailors with them must steer about.
If it were not for the Sailors we should never get a cup of tea,
Nor as little a pound of sugar to sweeten it wi'*. [with]
Nor as little people would get tobacco or snuff,
Nor as little would the ladies get a silk gown or a muff.
And many other good articles I need not mention,
For Carpenters to build ships it was a good invention.
I hope Sailors will be men that shall never stand idle;
And when they are upon the seas I'll hope they read their Bible.
They will mind* how Jesus to Peter stretched out his hand,
It was upon the seas, it was not upon land, [remember]
They will remember how Christ taught out of a ship,
And never let true religion out of their minds to slip,
I hope sailors will always believe on God's beloved Son,
For with both sea and land we will soon be done.
Every well-thinking person for Sailors should pray,
For their lawful calling makes them in danger every day.
That pleasant, beloved minister, Mr Brand,
Often prayed for them that was far from land.
When Sailors leave their friends at home,
I hope they'll be mindful of them when to sea they're gone.
I hope people will mind when Jonah out of the fish did pray,
Both by sea and land make God our all-sufficient stay.
Now you Carpenters and Sailors I bid you all adieu,
I wish God's blessing may be always with you.
Read Boston and Wilson [Willison] and William Dyer,
Of these three authors I think you'll never tire.
I hope these Scriptures we will all understand,
For we know not whether our call may be by sea or by land.

Janet Reid, 1839. [See the earliest broadside on page 8]

ON THE GALLANT SHOEMAKERS

[1] Let us have ever so many braw* clothes, [fine]
[2] Without shoes we would have very cold toes.
Everyone must live by their trade,
Shoemakers to people are very well bred.
If at any time a hole into the shoes does break out,
The Shoemakers will take them back and put on a clout*. [patch]
[7] Although we have braw shoes we should not have pride,
[8] For they just grow upon the cows' and horses' side.
[9] It must be steep'd among the bark that grows upon the tree,
[10] Ere ever it can be answerable for either you or me.
The curriers, with their knives, gives it a proper scrape;
After which the Shoemaker makes them both firm and neat.
[13] If leather shoes Ladies do not please,
[14] They can make them of the cloth that makes the claes*. [clothes]
[15] But for all this they must be firm with leather below,
[16] Or to the street the finest Lady could not go.
I hope people will their shoes well use,
And the Sabbath evening with them will not abuse.
At their own houses I hope they will appear,
And meditate upon what they did hear.
Shoemakers with wind and weather cannot be beat,
For they win their bread in their own house upon a seat.
[23] I hope Shoemakers will be men that are devout,
[24] I expect they will never wear the drunkard's coat.
[25] I trust Shoemakers will have good plans,
[26] And set a good example before young ones.
[27] Young people's minds are ready to be full of vanity;
[28] But the youngest and gayest death cannot defy.
Young and old – everyone – both rich and poor,
Must some day or night come to a dying hour.
Now all you Gallant Shoemakers, I bid you all adicu;
This was written in the year Eighteen Hundred and Thirty-Nine,
for you.

Janet Reid, 1839. [The numbered lines become the first 16 lines of *On the Shoemakers* on page 110]

ON THE MID-MILL

There is a spinning-mill stands in a howe*, [hollow]
The outside wheel with water round about does row*. [roll]
There dwells a family of very good respect,
And that the poor's case they never do neglect.
Respectable people often told me to go there,
For that was a family that always had something to spare.
Now at last into Mid-Mill I did go;
What people said I found it to be so.
Mid-Mill people, when I did go, were very kind to me,
And very much agreeableness amongst that people I did see.
Them that to the poor does give unto the Lord does lend,
And He in his own time and way will pay it back again.
Altho' our blessed Saviour the kingdom of heaven did merit,
He says, him that does the hungry feed and the naked clead*, shall it inherit. [clothe]
There's three verses in the fourteenth chapter of St Luke,
That Mid-Mill people and others read in their Holy Book.
I hope them and other Christians will be recompensed at the resurrection of the Just,
When this world and the fashion of it is all gone and past.
Mid-Mill people appeared all agreeable to be,
I hope young and old every day their Bibles do see.
Between beginning and amen many a pleasant word within,
I hope people will read their Bibles and keep away from sin.
Ere ever the year 'Forty comes round again,
There none of us on earth will likely remain.
We should all, rich and poor, learn contented to be,
For many is the alteration young and old every year do see.
I'm not now able the harvest for to shear;
I thank the public for many a penny and half-penny to me they do spare.
Now Mid-Mill people and all other Christians I bid you farewell,
I wish God's blessings on all Christians where ever they do dwell.

Janet Reid, 1840. [See both sides of the broadside overleaf]

ON THE MID-MILL.

There is a spinning-mill stands in a howe,
The outside wheel with water round about does row;
There dwells a family of very good respect,
And that the poor's case they never do neglect.
Respectable people often told me to go there,
For that was a family that had always something to spare.
Now at last into mid-mill I did go,
What people said I found it to be so;
Mid-mill people, when I did go, were very kind to me,
And very much agreeableness amongst that people I did see.
Them that to the poor does give unto the Lord does lend,
And he in his own time and way will pay it back again.
Altho' our blessed Saviour the kingdom of heaven did merit,
He says, him that does the hungry feed, and the naked clead,
shall it inherit.
There's three verses in the fourteenth chapter of Luke,
That mid-mill people and others read in their holy book.
I hope them and other Christians will be recompensed at the
resurrection of the just,
When this world and the fashion of it is all gone and past.
Mid-mill people appeared all agreeable to be.
I hope young and old every day their bibles do see,
Between beginning and amen many a pleasant word within,
I hope people will read their bibles and keep away from sin.
E're ever the year forty comes round again,
There none of us on earth will likely remain.
We should all, rich and poor, learn contented to be,
For many is the alteration young and old every year do see.
I'm not now able the harvest for to shear,
I thank the public for many a penny and half-penny to me
they do spare.
Now mid-mill people and all other Christians I bid you farewell,
I wish God's blessings on all Christians where ever they do dwell.

JANET REID, Carnock.

BAIRD, PRINTER, 174, TRONGATE, GLASGOW.

Peter Forbes' album. *Printed by Hugh Baird, Glasgow, 1840.*
[*See the poem on page 53*]

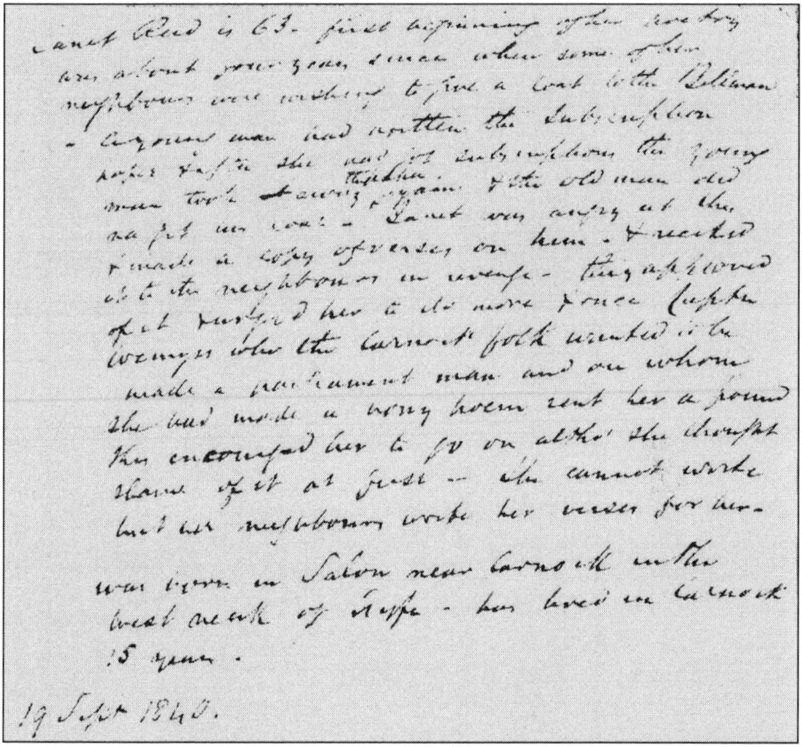
Janet Reid is 63 - first beginning of her poetry
was about four years since when some of her
neighbours were wishing to give a coat to the Bellman
- [illegible] man had written the subscription
paper & as she was got subscriptions the young
man took [illegible] away again & the old man did
not get his coat - Janet was angry at this
& made a copy of verses on him - & recited
it to the neighbours in revenge - they applauded
[illegible] her to do more since [illegible]
[illegible] when the Carnock folk wanted to be
made a parliament man and on whom
she had made a song poem sent her a pound
this encouraged her to go on altho' she thought
shame of it at first - she cannot write
but her neighbours write her verses for her -
was born in Salon near Carnock in the
west neuk of Fife - has lived in Carnock
15 years.

19 Sept 1840.

This is the broadside of *On the Mid-Mill* by Janet Reid printed by Hugh Baird in Glasgow in 1840 which was found in Peter Forbes' album. It has a pencil note written at its foot: '*See other side*'. This broadside is tipped in (pasted at the top of the broadside unlike the other broadsides in this album which are stuck down on all sides) and it has creases at the top from being raised. Written in pen and ink on the other side is this note. A previous owner of the album has typed a partial transcription which is tucked loose into the album. A full transcription of this note is given on page 13.

This note is dated 19 Sept 1840 and judging from Janet Reid's poem *On Pretty Paisley* Janet almost certainly arrived in Paisley on 15 September 1840, so this broadside was sold by her in Paisley. Janet must have told this story of her life to the unknown purchaser of this broadside who wrote it down that same day.

ON GLASGOW, BONNY TOWN
or ON GLASGOW'S BONNY CITY

First when I came into Glasgow town,
Very respectable people did me own.
It's a great sign their Bibles they do often read,
When unto strangers they do take heed.
I soon went over by Broomielaw,
On a great acquaintance there for to ca' *. [call]
That family was very discreet* to me, [obliging]
And very much discretion in that family I did see.
They of me, a stranger, did take great care,
And good lodgings for me they did prepare.
They took me to a widow, who was sober and douse*, [respectable]
And I lived very comfortable with her in her own house.
I have travelled in Glasgow through many a street,
And the people of Glasgow to me were always discreet.
In a short time I must bid bonny Glasgow farewell;
I wish God's blessings on Glasgow people to dwell.
I hope there are many of God's people in Glasgow do stay,
To the heavenly Zion are always seeking their way.
In a few short years there will come a new generation;
I wish they may never bring themselves nor their friends vexation*.
I trust they will read Christ's Sermon on the Mount, [sorrow]
And every one of their actions at it point.
I hope they will read the fourteenth and fifteenth of St John,
And the tenth of Hebrews often look upon.
Now about Glasgow, bonny town, I have little more to say –
Mind the poor, and keep Holy the Sabbath day.
I hope poor people will always be content,
And thank God for every blessing that is sent.
Now, for a time, I must bid bonny Glasgow adieu,
My Glasgow friends, this was written in the year Eighteen Hundred
and Forty, for you.

Janet Reid, 1840.

ON PRETTY PAISLEY

The people of Glasgow and Paisley are very smart,
They can bring in meal and potatoes without horse or cart;
If people in my young days had been so smart,
They would have sworn over them they had the black art;
It's a great pleasure to see the bonnie coaches reek*, [smoke]
But it is a cruel thing to see men the poor horses for to whip;
It surely was a good invention,
Who of the railway first did mention.
If people have money and time to spare,
They can soon go as far as Air*, [Ayr]
And if they have to hurry back,
The railway brings them in a crack.
If the poor have a sixpence, they cannot be beat,
For they can get in the coach altho' it has not seat.
It is a great convenience for both rich and poor,
I hope it will be a long time ere it be given o'er.
All earthly works must drop at the last day,
And I hope Paisley folks will ne'er forget to pray.
When in Paisley I was in a praying house,
With a respectable woman both sober and douse*. [respectable]
I went three times to church on Sabbath day,
And neighbours met at night with them to pray.
As long's I live I will remember
I went to pretty Paisley on the fifteenth of September.
I hope Paisley people ever will advise
The young and youthful to be wise,
And may they spend their days in grace,
And may their latter end be peace.

Janet Reid, 1840. [See the broadside on page 158]

ON THE YEAR 1841.

This is now another New Year,
And many of us on earth doth yet appear.
We should all learn contented for to be,
For many is the alteration every year we see.
There's but a meeting here, and to part again—
It's but a few short years any of us will on earth remain
We should all mind what our Saviour did say—
For we know not the hour nor the day·
In our short day we should never be idle,
but always employed about our Bible.
We should all avoid Martha's care,
And for the soul more than the body prepare.
Remember what our Saviour to Mary did say—
"The part that she had chosen would not be taken away."
Rich and poor should mind God's word,
For it is sharper than any two-edged sword.
The 12th Chapter of John we should often read,
And there we'll see our Saviour's humble deed.
Of houses there is many a pretty raw,
E'er the year 40 comes again, Death will give them a ca'
Though the gates be made of stronger metal than clay,
For all this Death through them will find his way.
The 25 Chapter of Matthew we should never forget,
And mind that out of all our earthly dwellings we all must flit
Ere ever the year 40 comes round again,
There's none of us on earth will likely remain,
The rich and poor, and every one.
That wishes to follow the religious plan,
Should read their Testaments, Old and New,
And they will teach every one how to do.

JANET REID, Carnock.

National Library of Scotland, Edinburgh. [*No printer's imprint – possibly printed in Falkirk*] *1841.*

ON THE YEAR 1841

This is now another New Year,
And many of us on earth doth yet appear.
We should all learn contented for to be,
For many is the alteration every year we see.
There's but a meeting here, and to part again –
It's but a few short years any of us will on earth remain.
We should all mind what our Saviour did say –
For we know not the hour nor the day.
In our short day we should never be idle,
But always employed about our Bible.
We should all avoid Martha's care,
And for the soul more than the body prepare.
Remember what our Saviour to Mary did say –
'The part that she had chosen would not be taken away.'
Rich and poor should mind God's word,
For it is sharper than any two-edged sword.
The twelfth chapter of St John we should often read,
And there we'll see our Saviour's humble deed.
Of houses there is many a pretty raw*, [row]
Ere the year 'Forty comes again, Death will give them a ca'*. [call]
Though the gates be made of stronger metal than clay,
For all this Death through them will find his way.
The twenty-fifth chapter of St Matthew we should never forget,
And mind that out of all our earthly dwellings we all must flit.
Ere ever the year 'Forty comes round again,
There's none of us on earth will likely remain.
The rich and poor, and everyone
That wishes to follow the religious plan,
Should read their Testaments, Old and New,
And they will teach everyone how to do.

Janet Reid, 1841.

JANET REID would have visited and would probably have stayed in Stirling in early 1841 before she reached Bridge of Allan but no poems have been found composed by her while she was staying in Stirling; and none of her broadsides have been found printed for her in Stirling in 1841. While Janet stayed or lived in Bridge of Allan she always used the Stirling Observer Office to print her broadsides and she probably went there once a month. The Stirling Observer Office was at 38 Baker Street, Stirling, until sometime in 1843 when it moved to 20 and 22 Murray Place, Stirling.

The collection of 35 broadsides by Janet Reid was found in a specially-bound album entitled *Rhymes by Janet Reid, Carnock* with the bookplate of a Peter Forbes who appeared to have 'borrowed' the crest of the Forbes' family. There are 90 'Peter Forbes' in the 1891 national census and one of them must have written the note to Erskine Beveridge in 1894 which accompanied the 36th broadside. How did Peter Forbes obtain so many broadsides?

John Forbes of Stirling edited and published *The Tourist's Companion Through Stirling* (1847) and it has his advertisement as an auctioneer at 35 Baker Street, Stirling. The national census of 1851 records that John Forbes was also a bookseller and his advertisements in *The Stirling Observer* in the 1840s show that his bookshop was at 35 Baker Street, Stirling. The most likely person to have accumulated 36 broadsides may have been a bookseller.

Could a link be found between John Forbes of Stirling and one of these 90 'Peter Forbes'? John Henderson, a former Scottish primary school headteacher who advised me on Scottish culture and helped me with genealogical research, found these details of John Forbes in the Statutory Register of Deaths (SRD) and in the censuses:

> SRD: John Forbes, formerly 'bookbinder master', parents Adam Forbes a 'Chelsea pensioner' (soldier with 20 years' service) and Mary Horky Bain, widower of Rachel Syme, died in 1871 aged 76 in Stirling, informant being his son, William Syme Forbes.
>
> 1871 census: John Forbes aged 76, born in Lybster, Latheron, Caithness, son William aged 45 'book binder', William's wife Mary aged 40 (born St Mary's Wynd, Stirling) and son William aged 22 'blacksmith', living in 33 St Mary's Wynd, Stirling.

> 1861 census: John Forbes aged 65, born in Latheron, Caithness, 'bookseller master employing one man', son William aged 35 'bookseller master journeyman', William's wife Mary aged 40 and son William aged 15, living in 23 St John Street, Stirling.
>
> 1851 census: John Forbes aged 55 widower, 'book seller and auctioneer', living in Spittal Street, Stirling.
>
> 1841 census: John Forbes aged 45 'book seller', wife Rachel aged 45, children John aged 20 'book binder', William aged 15 'book binder apprentice' and Mary aged 15 (these ages are rounded down to the nearest 5 years) living in Baker Street, Stirling.

The Peter Forbes who wrote the note to Erskine Beveridge (Junior) in 1894 appears to have been elderly so probably he was one of the oldest of the 90 'Peter Forbes' in the 1891 census:

Age	Residence	Occupation	Place of Birth
57	Newington, Edinburgh	Joiner	Moulin, Perthshire
58	Killin, Perth	Gamekeeper	Fortingall, Perthshire
58	Cockpen, Midlothian	Inspector of Poor clerk	Pitlochry, Perthshire
58	Ardoch, Perth	General lab.	Ardoch, Perthshire
58	Kinning Park, Glasgow	Engine keeper	Auchendore, Aberdeenshire
60	Portsoy, Banff	Retired farmer	Fordyce, Banffshire
66	St George, Edinburgh	Fisherman	Latheron, Caithness
73	Strathdon, Aberdeen	Former sheep dealer	Lowie, Aberdeenshire
77	Wick, Caithness	Former lab.	Reay, Caithness
79	Moulin, Perth	Retired quarryman	Moulin, Perthshire
84	Reay, Caithness	Pauper	Reay, Caithness

John Henderson searched for these and found details of the Peter Forbes aged 66 living in the St George district of Edinburgh in 1891 in the Statutory Register of Deaths (SRD) and in the censuses:

> SRD: Peter Forbes, parents Peter Forbes 'fisherman' and Isabella Forbes, widower of Elizabeth Sutherland, died in 1907 aged 82 in Edinburgh, informant being his son, Thomas Forbes.

Continued

1891 census: Peter Forbes aged 66 'fisherman' born Latheron, Caithness, wife Elizabeth aged 65, children Peter aged 30 a 'sculptor', and grandson Thomas aged 12, living in 3 Caledonian Crescent [St George district], Edinburgh.

1881 census: Peter Forbes aged 56 'salmon fisher', born Lybster, wife Elizabeth aged 53 born Wick, children Peter aged 20, Margaret aged 16, George aged 14, and grandson Thomas aged 2, all born in Lybster, living in 136 Russell Street, Edinburgh.

1871 census: Peter Forbes aged 46 born Latheron, Caithness, wife Elizabeth aged 42, children Thomas aged 13, Peter aged 10, Margaret aged 6 and George aged 4, living in Lybster, Latheron, Caithness.

Lybster (which had the third largest herring-fishing fleet in Scotland at this time) near Latheron, Caithness, in the north-east of Scotland is where both Peter Forbes (aged 66 in the 1891 census) and John Forbes (aged 76 in the 1871 census) were born. So they were probably related and Peter Forbes (aged 66 in 1891) of St George, Edinburgh, most likely possessed the album and most likely wrote the note to Erskine Beveridge in 1894. Possibly Peter's father was John's brother and they were nephew and uncle. So Peter Forbes was probably given the broadsides by John Forbes' son, William, when he found them in his father's effects after his father's death in 1871. William (a 'bookbinder') probably specially bound the album and pasted the 36 (now 35) broadsides inside it.

But John Forbes's wife Rachel Syme was probably the original collector of these broadsides (the latest one being *Milsey Bank Female School* printed in 1844). Rachel's death after a long illness was announced in *The Stirling Observer* on 13 September 1849. Perhaps Rachel met Janet Reid selling her broadsides in Stirling in 1843 and bought the nine broadsides that Janet carried with her that day which had just been printed in the same batch in the Stirling Observer Office. Perhaps Rachel found the other broadsides among her husband's stock. But Rachel did not meet Janet again or she would have bought even more! So John Forbes kept these broadsides, collected by his wife Rachel Syme, without adding to them after her death in 1849 until he died in 1871.

ON AIRTHREY WATER

Airthrey Water is both clean and clear,
But not so pleasant to the taste as a bottle of good beer.
There is many things that are unpleasant to the taste,
But they are counted very good for a digest.
While wood does grow, and swallows does fly,
I hope the wholesome Wells o' Airthrey will never run dry.
At Airthrey Wells, from all quarters many a one does meet,
And strangers to one another there are always discreet;
Perhaps marriages there may be made up,
While they of Airthrey Water does take a cup.
We all know that marriage is no sin,
For with the first man and woman marriage did begin;
And while this world does endure,
Marriages will always be and that we're sure.
Marriage is only for this life,
And it's not ordained for every woman to be a wife.
The woman that seven husbands had,
The grave at last became her bed.
We should always set our hearts beyond the grave,
Where through Christ's sufferings pleasures evermore we may have.
The thoughts of a better world should be often in our mind,
For this world, and all that's in't, we must soon leave behind.
God grant that through Christ's merit one another we may see,
Where sun or moon there will never need to be.
We should often think of Christ's wondrous love,
And should always set our hearts on things above;
For that to us was his great desire,
That of religious matters we should never tire.
Airthrey Water is a very useful spring,
But the Water of Life is surely a better thing.
The waters of Airthrey may not always cure,
But the Water of Life stand for ever sure.
My Brig o'Allan strangers, I wish you all well,
And I wish God's blessing may rest on you wherever you do dwell.

Janet Reid, 1841.

ON DUNBLANE.

The bonny little Town of Dumblane,
Is a pleasant little place and stands alane,
There the old Cathedral you will see,
It is admired by many, as well as by me.
This is a very distressing time indeed,
I hope the rich will mind the poors' need,
When working people work they cannot get,
Them and their families must solitary sit.
I trust the rich will the poors' case consider;
Few working people can help sister or brother.
If working people work again should find,
To make good use of their money, I hope, they will be inclined;
I hope they will never again fill the gill stoup and had it clinkin',
At such worthless ways they will take a winkin'.
The waters of Dunblane are clean and clear,
But the price of liquor many visitors does never speir,
I hope Dunblane folk will give one another a good advice,
We should all strive to learn to be wise,
I hope they will often meet with one another to pray.
None will ever rue that when come to a dying day.
Dunblane for ministers has the advantage of many a place,
I hope them and their strangers will daily grow in grace,
I trust you will take a turn on mount calvary every day;
Remember how our Saviour for us did bleed and pray;
Often think of Christ's sufferings in the garden and on the tree,
How he suffered for sinners such as you and me.
While wood does grow, and swallows does fly,
I hope the wells of Dunblane will ne'er run dry.
I trust many a Christian does there abide,
And, for ought I know, many of them in their coach do ride.

JANET REID, CARNOCK.

1842.

Gilchrist, Printer, Glasgow.

Mitchell Library, Glasgow. *Printed by William Gilchrist, Glasgow, 1842.*

ON DUNBLANE

The bonny little Town of Dunblane,
Is a pleasant little place and stands alane.
There the old Cathedral you will see,
It is admired by many, as well as by me.
This is a very distressing time indeed,
I hope the rich will mind the poor's need.
When working people work they cannot get,
Them and their families must solitary sit.
I trust the rich the poor's case consider;
Few working people can help sister or brother.
If working people work again should find,
To make good use of their money, I hope, they will be inclined;
I hope they will never again fill the gill stoup and had it clinkin',
At such worthless ways they will take a winkin'.
The waters of Dunblane are clean and clear,
But the price of liquor many visitors does never spear*, [question]
I hope Dunblane folk will give one another good advice,
We should all strive to learn to be wise,
I hope they will often meet with one another to pray,
None will ever rue that when come to a dying day.
Dunblane for ministers has the advantage of many a place,
I hope them and their strangers will grow daily in grace.
I trust you will take a turn on Mount Calvary every day;
Remember how our Saviour for us did bleed and pray;
Often think of Christ's sufferings in the Garden and on the Tree,
How he suffered for sinners such as you and me.
While woods does grow and swallows does fly,
I hope the Wells* of Dunblane will ne'er run dry. [Springs]
I trust many a Christian does there abide,
And, for ought I know, many of them in their coach do ride.

Janet Reid, 1841.

IN SPEAKING BE MILD

Mind pure religion and undefiled,
And unto one another be always mild.
Mind what Joseph to his brethren did say –
See that ye fall not out by the way;
Remember Joshua who was sober and douse*, [respectable]
Let everyone remember themselves and their own house;
We should always remember our own beam,
And in every season we should look at hame*; [home]
Remember what our Saviour to the people did say,
Them that are without sin throw the first stone away;
We should always look down to our own black feet,
And about our neighbour's fault we should never leet*; [list]
The Ten Commandments are all in force,
Never break the ninth to make our neighbour worse;
The scriptures they do often say,
That evil speaking should be always put away;
Everyone off their neighbours should hold their tongue,
And especially those that have families that are young;
There is sometimes much between the cradle and the grave,
None know how their own offspring may behave;
We should always be giving one another a good advice,
All, and every one of us, should learn to be wise;
We should always meet with one another to pray,
None will ever rue that when they come to a dying day;
Young and old, and everyone – both rich and poor –
Must one day or night come to a dying hour.
Good People, read the one hundred and thirtieth Psalm,
And to one another be always kind and calm;
Them that do Christianity profess,
Against their neighbours' faults should never guess.

Janet Reid, 1841.

ON THE YEAR FORTY-TWO

This is now another New Year,
And many of us on earth doth yet appear.
We should all learn contented for to be,
For many an alteration every year we see.
In our short day we should never be idle,
But very often employed at our Bible.
The scriptures we should all understand,
For we may soon get our call by sea or by land.
We should set our hearts beyond the grave,
As we know not, on earth, how few days we may have.
Remember what our Saviour to Mary did say –
The part she had chosen would ne'er be taken away.
Often think of Christ's sufferings in the Garden and on the Tree –
How he suffered for sinners such as you and me.
The first chapter of Proverbs you will read,
And remember that God sees every deed.
Mind what our Saviour, while on earth, he did say –
We must give account for every idle word at the Judgement Day.
To many a one it's a sore vexation*, [sorrow]
At present to think of so many in starvation.
When working people work they cannot get,
Sure them and their family solitary sit.
The year 'Forty-One is now past and gone,
We should all thank God for meat to eat, and clothing to put on.
It is now come in the year 'Forty-Two –
We trust there will be meat to eat and plenty of work to do.
There's many a misty morning turned out a bonny day,
We hope that dull trade from the land will soon pass away.
Good people, to righteousness I hope you will incline,
And God will bring relief to you in his own way and time.

Janet Reid, 1842.

MELANCHOLY ACCIDENT

The *Telegraph*, new high pressure engine steam boat,
When not far from Helensburgh Quay did float;
A melancholy accident has been,
The like about this place before was never seen.
This Steamer and the Railroad, I understand, were trying a race;
People for gain one another should never chase.
If people cannot gain a sixpence, they should be content with a groat;
For it is sometimes dangerous when folks on the water do float.
By what our Saviour at the Tower of Siloam did say,
We should speak cautiously, let the case be what it may.
As the tree falleth, so must it lie;
To lead a righteous life everybody should try.
There are many in Glasgow and Greenock now will weep,
When they think that friends and acquaintances in death doth sleep.
I hope many of their friends hereafter will see,
Where sun nor moon will ever need to be.
This happened in the year Eighteen Hundred and Forty-Two,
When folks about railways and steamers made so much ado.
When in the mornings people do rise,
Sometimes ere night they meet a sad surprise;
And many a one has gone well to bed at night,
And never again hath seen the morning light.
Oh, may we all remember, every day,
That time with everyone is flying fast away.
The fourteenth and fifteenth Paraphrase I advise you to read,
And with sober people always take up your head.
The Scriptures we should all try to understand,
For we know not whether our call may be by sea or land.
It was on March twenty-first, the boiler of this steamer at
Helensburgh did burst,
When worthy Captain Ewing, with the gallant crew and passengers,
into the sea were thrust.
We should always set our hearts beyond the grave,
Where through Christ's sufferings pleasures we evermore may have.

Janet Reid, 1842. [See the broadside on page 144]

AGAINST SABBATH BREAKERS

The thirty-first of Exodus, the first of Proverbs, and fifty-eighth of
Isaiah read,
And mingle with sober people in every deed.
Psalm second, fiftieth, and likewise ninety-fort,
And with Sabbath keepers always resort.
What would many heathen nations give
For the gospel blessings under which we live.
Each Sabbath in the church we all should meet,
If none of us or our near friends be sick.
The Canal Company never did yet make attempt
Any person from the House of God to prevent.
The Railway Company know that the world is very loose,
And they wish to give all Sabbath breakers scouth*. [scope]
The Sabbath none of us should ever profane;
None will ever be enriched by Sabbath gain.
The death of the righteous, people would surely wish to die,
And none of us God's laws should ever defy.
People in my young days surely had not been so frail,
For they never went by railway coach nor mail*, [mail-coach]
But to hear sermon 10 or 12 miles would have walked on fit,
And contentedly all day on the green grass did sit.
For all that ministers and good men do say,
People will go by rails and mails on Sabbath day.
The Ten Commandments are all yet in force,
People should never break the fourth to make the country worse.
I hope her Majesty will agree in this with me,
No Sabbath's winnings will ever wish to hear of or see.
Our female sex was the first that made man to sin,
And we should be diligent to bring Sabbath breakers in.
Read the second verse of the third chapter of Malachi,
In the end of the Old Testament you will it see.
But a few Sabbaths the longest liver will be here,
Before Christ's judgment-seat rich and poor must all appear.

Janet Reid, 1842.

THE Old Brig o' Allan was built in 1520 at a ford over the Allan Water. Ella MacLean writes in *Bridge of Allan: The Rise of a Village* (1970) that the Old Brig was: 'Stone-built, narrow, and hog-backed, rising sharply from the river bank and dipping steeply to the other side'. The Old Brig was restored in 1638 and again in 1697 and it was: 'Heightened, widened and strengthened' in 1842 when a third arch was built for the lade (mill-stream) on the western bank. Bridge of Allan, which now stands astride the Allan Water, arose from seven clachans (hamlets): Old Lecropt, Keirfield, Bridge End, Miln of Airthrey, Pathfoot, Logie and Cornton.

Robert Chambers in *The Picture of Scotland* (1827) describes Bridge of Allan as: 'Soft, sunny, warm – a confusion of straw-roofed cottages and rich mossy trees; possessed of a bridge and a mill, together with kail-yards [cabbage-plots], bee-skeps, colleys [dogs], callants [lads], old inns with entertainment for man and horse, carts with their poles pointing up to the sky, venerable dames in drugget, knitting their stockings in the sun, and young ones in gingham and dimity, tripping along with milk-pails on their heads'.

The Mine House was built in 1738 for the copper-miners and later it provided lodgings for visitors. The Well House and the Pump Room were built over the old mine shaft in 1821 by Sir Robert Abercromby and the Bath House was built close by in 1829.

In 1826 Robert Stevenson, lighthouse engineer and grandfather of Robert Louis Stevenson, arched the mine passage and piped the Airthrey Water 1,000 feet from the springs in the copper mine to a cistern and then up the old mine shaft to the Pump Room. He built fourteen timber platforms in the old mine shaft. Charles Roger (later Rogers) in *A Week at Bridge of Allan* (1851-59) writes that: 'The shaft, which is thirty fathoms deep [one fathom is 6 feet], is provided by a series of ladders, fastened on platforms, at safe distances, by means of which the mine may be explored'. Any amount of Airthrey Water could be drunk in the Pump Room for two (old) pence.

George Dixon in 'The Founding Decade of Modern Bridge of Allan, 1836-45' published in *The Forth Naturalist and Historian* (2004) writes that in 1836 Captain Henderson had plots of land laid out in Bridge of Allan. The first 13 plots were feued (leased) in 1837 and the first new villas were built that same year.

ON AIRTHREY WELL HOUSE

The people here keep baths of different kinds three,
Which will answer people of high or low degree;
Likewise good lodgings for visitors they do prepare,
The strangers in good usage they will always share;
And they can take a walk around the house,
And the people that belong to it are always sober and douse.
The strangers can walk about at their leisure,
And pull a bonny flower at their pleasure;
There they can pull the brier that grows so sweet,
And the people there, and strangers, are always discreet;
And in the corner there grows a bonny bunch of honeysuckle,
Perhaps young people there in marriage may buckle.
It's long since marriage was the fashion in our Scotch land,
And likewise in England as we do understand.
When people comes about this country,
Perhaps a choice for themselves they may see;
And if it be their fortune for to be wed,
To see them comfortable I will be very glad.
I must now turn to the house that near the Well* does stand, [Spring]
And the master and mistress has servants at their command;
Likewise a pretty daughter that they lead in their hand –
This child is but young yet, as we do understand.
I hope this child will grow in grace,
And be an honour to all her friends about the place.
This child may yet be a lady,
And I hope she will get a husband when once she is ready.
I hope her parents will set before her a good example,
And if she lives till she is old she will likely keep the sample.
Her parents are both of very good respect,
And the poor and needy's case they never do neglect.
The strangers will see this bonny house as they pass by,
And it is a bonny house no strangers will deny.
The six corners of the house I cannot get in,
And to spoil my poem I need not begin.

Janet Reid, 1842. [See the broadside on page 137]

ON 20 July 1842 *The Scotsman*, an Edinburgh daily newspaper, published a report under the heading 'Bridge of Allan' mentioning Janet Reid in which the newspaper correspondent is probably making fun of her Fife accent. The two lines of the poem quoted are almost certainly the opening lines of another poem by Janet about Bridge of Allan that has not been found. That a 'red-coated colonel' was regarded as Janet's 'formidable rival', may indicate that Janet too wore red – like the 'petticoat o' crimson hue' that Edith MacAlpine of Limekilns recalls her wearing in Carnock:

> This delightful watering-place is very gay at present with visitors, chiefly from Edinburgh and Glasgow. Besides the Airthrie Spring, so celebrated for its medicinal virtues, medicated vapour-baths have been recently opened. [...] The water-drinkers assemble about seven in the morning, when tumbler after tumbler is discussed with the most approved tee-total resoluteness. After breakfast, parties betake themselves to fishing excursions on the Allan, the Teith, and the Forth, or, better still, ascend one or other of the neighbouring hills, where a view is obtained which for grandeur of scenery is scarcely surpassed by any in Europe. [...] On Saturday week a concert was given in the new Reading-Room [and Music Hall, a building which was demolished in 1902 and not the 'Reading-Room' of Janet Reid's poem *On the Reading-Room*] [...] after which a ball was given to those frequenting the Wells, which went off with great spirit under the auspices of Captain Henderson [not yet promoted to Major], proprietor of a fine range of cottages lately built. [...] The officers of the 42nd, at present in Stirling Castle, were present, the piper of the regiment parading the principal street of the village. Janet Reid, the Carnock *potess* [sic], is plying a rich harvest here selling her penny *pottery* [sic]. Two lines will suffice –
>
> > The Bridge of Allan is a bonnie place,
> > Where you will see many a comely and pretty face!
>
> The red-coated colonel, however, with his fife [flute], is a formidable rival to honest Janet, who, on being asked what she thought of [Robert] Burns, said: 'Nae doubt Burns had been a kind o' clever; but he was ower fine wi' his poetry. What was the use o' folk being sae particular!'

ON THE BONNY BRIG O'ALLAN

It is a bonny place the Brig o' Allan,
And with improvement it's daily swallin'*; [swelling]
A good addition is now made to the Brig,
And there wi'* pleasure coaches may ride. [with]
If any one wishes there to take a jaunt,
Good lodgings there they never will want;
The people there and strangers are of good respect,
The poor and needy's case they never do neglect;
Many ones [come] from the east and west and from the south and north, [Meanderings]
And many a one comes sailing up the bonny Links* of Forth;
There they can take a walk among the trees so green,
Where many of God's wonders may be thought upon or seen.
There is three verses in the fourteenth chapter of St Luke,
That Christians will see in that Holy Book.
The Charitable will be recompensed at the resurrection of the Just,
After this world is all gone and past.
When so many to the Brig o' Allan do repair,
For to drink the mineral waters and to get the callar* air; [bracing]
When for our bodily health we have so great respect,
I hope for our soul's health we never will neglect.
Before to the Well* of Airthrey good people does come in, [Spring]
On the left side of the road you'll see a new town begin.
No doubt it was sin that has made man to mourn,
And many a one for want through the country takes a turn.
Good people, I hope you will read the second chapter of St James,
And be kind to people when away from their hames.
Likewise the thirteenth chapter of St John,
And the poor's case I hope you will often think upon.
Many a one is forced to beg their bread from door to door,
And while the world stands there always will be poor.
Many a one their whole lifetime it is sour,
It's surely best to eat the bran before the flour.

Janet Reid, 1842.

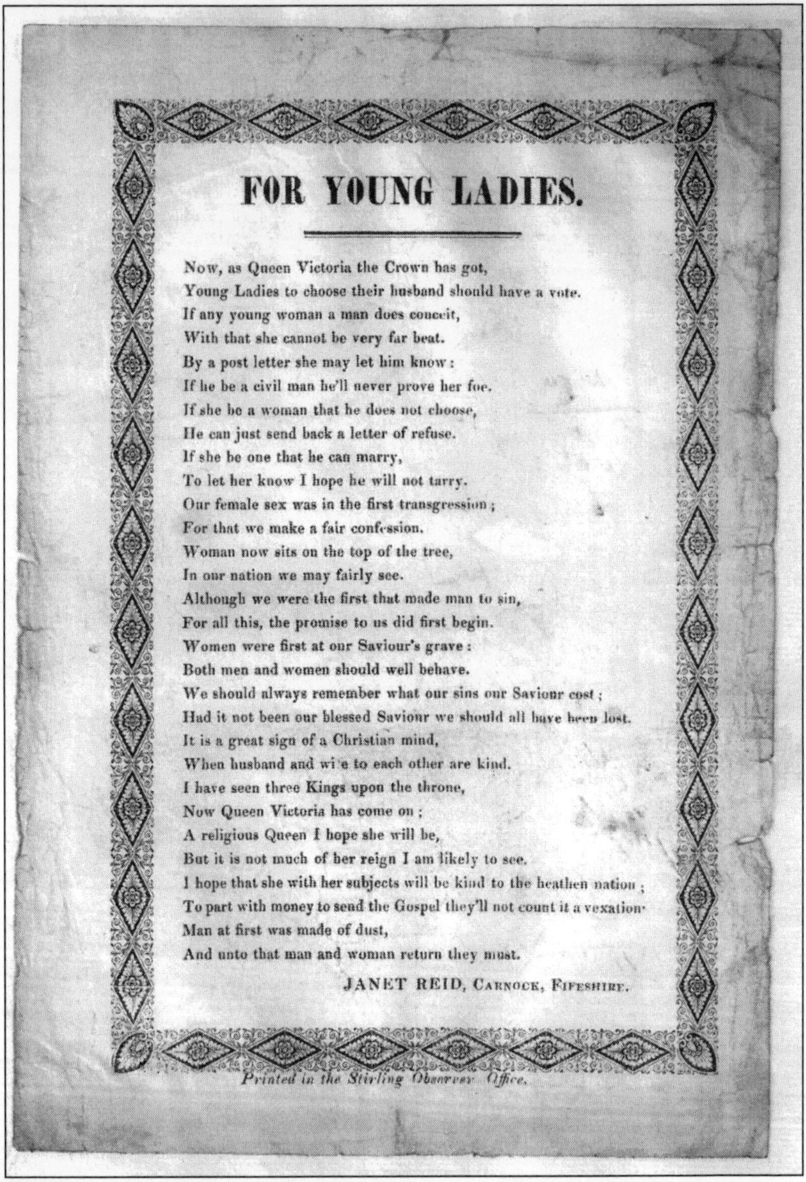

FOR YOUNG LADIES.

Now, as Queen Victoria the Crown has got,
Young Ladies to choose their husband should have a vote.
If any young woman a man does conceit,
With that she cannot be very far beat.
By a post letter she may let him know:
If he be a civil man he'll never prove her foe.
If she be a woman that he does not choose,
He can just send back a letter of refuse.
If she be one that he can marry,
To let her know I hope he will not tarry.
Our female sex was in the first transgression;
For that we make a fair confession.
Woman now sits on the top of the tree,
In our nation we may fairly see.
Although we were the first that made man to sin,
For all this, the promise to us did first begin.
Women were first at our Saviour's grave:
Both men and women should well behave.
We should always remember what our sins our Saviour cost;
Had it not been our blessed Saviour we should all have been lost.
It is a great sign of a Christian mind,
When husband and wife to each other are kind.
I have seen three Kings upon the throne,
Now Queen Victoria has come on;
A religious Queen I hope she will be,
But it is not much of her reign I am likely to see.
I hope that she with her subjects will be kind to the heathen nation;
To part with money to send the Gospel they'll not count it a vexation.
Man at first was made of dust,
And unto that man and woman return they must.

JANET REID, CARNOCK, FIFESHIRE.

Printed in the Stirling Observer Office.

Peter Forbes' album. *Printed in the Stirling Observer Office, 1843.*

FOR YOUNG LADIES

Now, as Queen Victoria the Crown has got,
Young Ladies to choose their Husbands should have a vote.
If any young woman a man does conceit*, [admire]
With that she cannot be very far beat.
By a post letter she may let him know,
If he be a civil man he'll never prove her foe.
If she be a woman that he does not choose,
He can just send back a letter of refuse.
If she be one that he can marry,
To let her know I hope he will not tarry.
Our female sex was in the first transgression,
For that we must make a fair confession.
Woman now sits at the top of the tree,
In our nation we may fairly see.
Although we were the first that made man to sin,
For all this, the promise to us did first begin.
Women were first at our Saviour's grave,
Both men and women should well behave.
We should always remember what our sins our Saviour cost,
Had it not been our blessed Saviour we should all have been lost.
It is a great sign of a Christian mind,
When husband and wife to each other are kind.
I have seen three Kings upon the throne,
Now Queen Victoria is comed on.
A religious Queen I hope she will be –
But it is not much of her reign I am likely to see.
I hope that she with her subjects will be kind to the heathen nation,
To part with money to send the Gospel they'll not count it a
vexation*. [sorrow]
Man at first was made of dust,
And unto that man and woman return they must.

Janet Reid, 1842.

FOR GENTLEMEN AND LADIES
or FOR LADIES AND GENTLEMEN

Young Ladies, we may all understand,
Have their freedom in our Scottish land.
Woman now, at this day, is at the head of our nation,
A young lady about a gentleman need not be in vexation*. [sorrow]
I think a lady in love would never do better,
Than send the gentleman a civil letter.
If the gentleman does no good, he'll do no ill –
A handsome lady's market he will never spill.
Everyone knows how their own shoes does them bind,
And to keep a lady's secret, a gentleman will be inclined.
It is a long time since love did begin,
And we all know that true love is no sin.
There's many a man does not know whose heart he has a keeping,
Although he did know, about that he will not be speaking.
I hope no young man will prove a woman's foe,
If ever he comes for to know.
If he can't return love again,
He will let no person ken*. [know]
We know how it was with Jacob of old –
True love by no person should be told.
What more is a woman than a man;
But she always tries to hide her love if she can.
Many a woman on her marriage day,
Her heart could go another way.
But it is not the fashion for women in our land,
To reveal their love to a man, as we do understand.
But this fashion in our land should be done away,
And women for a partner in life should get something to say.
They have their part in marriage up for to hold;
I think to speak or write they should be bold.
Although marriage is only for this life,
True love will make many a pleasant wife.
It's a pity any woman should be married against her mind;
Sometimes to marry another, a bride is inclined.

Janet Reid, 1842.

FOR BACHELORS

Bachelors, we all must understand,
Must surely be afraid to take a young Lady by the hand.
Bachelors must surely think much of their money,
That they are afraid to make a young Lady their honey.
If any man wishes to live comfortable through life,
He will take some pleasant young woman for his wife.
God said it was not good for man to be alone,
But that surely Bachelors never yet has known.
God said he would make for man a help that was meet,
But that help Bachelors never does seek.
I hope good people will understand,
That there is many a pleasant young Lady in the land.
A Bachelor for a young Lady might have a good seat,
And to take home a young lady he need not be very far beat.
I have set the young Ladies now on a plan,
To try for themselves to get a young man.
A long time have Kings been on the throne,
But now that time for Bachelors has gone.
It will be a long time ere ever we will have a King again;
I hope good luck with the Ladies all that time will remain.
I hope Gentlemen and Ladies will live a religious life,
And married or unmarried, I hope they will never live in strife;
For in our country there is many a pleasant wife.
Married or unmarried we contented should be,
For many alterations we every year do see.
Time with everyone is wearing away;
There will be neither marrying nor giving in marriage at the last day.
People's minds are ready to be full of vanity,
But neither rich nor poor can death defy.
Both young and old, rich and poor,
Must some day or night come to a dying hour.

Janet Reid, 1842.

MAJOR HENDERSON (1806-1858), who is mentioned by Janet Reid in some of her poems, was the driving force behind the rise of Bridge of Allan. John Erskine writes in *Erskine's Guide to Bridge of Allan 'Queen of the Scottish Spas'* (1901) that John Alexander took the name of his maternal uncle, Dr John Henderson, from whom he inherited the Westerton Estate in Bridge of Allan in 1822. John Alexander Henderson joined the army in Stirling in 1824 and he served for 20 years in India, Canada and on the Mediterranean. After his return to Bridge of Allan he lived at Westerton House and remained a bachelor. Major John Alexander Henderson 'late of the 4th Light Dragoons and Rifle Brigade' is buried in the Henderson family grave in the Old Kirkyard at Logie Old Kirk.

CHARLES ROGER (1825-1890) was the prime mover in raising funds to build the National Wallace Monument in 1861 on Abbey Craig near Bridge of Allan. A copy of his *A Week at Bridge of Allan* was placed in a crystal vase at the laying of its foundation stone.

He was born in Dunino near St Andrews, Fife, the son of a minister. His mother died in childbirth and he was brought up by his father's sister, Isabella Roger (born in 1793). Charles Roger is described as: 'A man of words [...] millions of words' by J. Malcolm Allan in 'Who Was Charles Rogers?' published in *The Forth Naturalist and Historian*, Volume 13: 1990. He married Isabella Smith Bain (1824-1880) of St Andrews, Fife, on 8 December 1854. The marriage took place in the bride's home as customary in Scotland at that time and there is no record other than the calling of the banns.

The entry in the Old Parish Register kept at New Logie Kirk is: '*1854 December 8th Dr Charles Rogers* [sic] *of this parish and Isabella Bain of the parish of St Andrews gave in their names for proclamation of Banns for one day*'. It was his responsibility to ensure that the names were correct at New Logie – so afterwards he changed his name to fit the banns! In the proclamation of the same banns in the Old Parish Register of St Andrews, his name is given as '*Rodgers'* but that was the Bain's mistake. In 1855 he was ordained chaplain to the Stirling Castle garrison which came with a salary of £74 and a free house. In *Leaves from My Autobiography* (1876) he writes: 'The appointment was welcome after a novitiate of nine years during which I had earned by preaching £266 16s 6d'.

ON AN ACCIDENT AT THE BRIG O'ALLAN

It was in the year Eighteen Hundred and Forty-Two on the
    eighteenth day of June,
This accident happened in that same forenoon;
This poor man that day lost part of his hand,
I hope good people will all understand.
He has a wife and children three,
In straightened circumstances they cannot but be.
They who do the hireling's wages keep up,
They do not know what may be in their own cup.
Whatever money is over paying the printer's fee,
To this poor family I intend all of it to gi'e*. [give]
There's many a generous person at Airthrey Well,
And I hope this little paper I soon will sell.
The twenty-fifth chapter of St Matthew you may read,
And it will show you how to do in many a deed.
Them who do their talents well improve,
The Lord of these servants did them love;
But him that did his talent in a napkin tie,
The Lord also did him deny.
The twenty-eighth Paraphrase, good people, you will often see,
And in deeds of charity there will pleasure be.
Cornelius's alms, as well as his prayers, did come
Before the Lord for a memorial of him.
Our blessed Saviour, he did say –
That the poor will be always in your way.
This man came to his poverty by no disgrace,
As is well known to everybody in the place.
I hope now everyone will charitable be,
Knowing that this poor man is not now able to win a fee.
Both rich and poor, and everyone
That wishes to follow the charity plan,
Read your Testaments, Old and New,
And that will teach everyone how to do.

Janet Reid, 1842.

ON VANITY FAIR

It was on the sixth day of August, in the year 'Forty-Two –
Such vanity as was acted not far from Stirling will not always do.
I think people may call it Vanity Fair,
To act such folly on Saturday should be very rare.
Such cruelty in a Christian land should not be,
To make the poor horses jump o'er a palin'* tree. [paling]
They should mind what Balaam's ass to him did say –
They should not beat poor horses so cruel on the way.
People should be merciful to every beast,
And not spend so much of their precious time in jest.
This is said to be the 'Chapmen's Race';
There appears there to be very little growth in grace.
The poor dumb beasts they do abuse,
And their own souls they do not well use –
To act such folly on Saturday afternoon,
But it will soon wear over their days of June.
Time with both man and woman is fast wearing away,
And it will not be long that any of us here on earth can stay.
We should always set our hearts beyond the grave,
Where through Christ's sufferings, pleasures ever more we may
have.
We should go to the Valley and hear righteous men preach and pray;
We should always keep out of sinners' way.
The little man his horse did sorely whip,
But off the ground the proud youth had to creep.
I think that he ne'er again will try a fence,
For if he does, he'll show his want of sense.
As for Saturday's races, I hope people will never chase,
In case they may find themselves worse than the beasts.
Now good people, I bid you adieu –
I believe this poem may not please some of you.

Janet Reid, 1842.

ON DRAPERS AND GROCERS

The Drapers can sell either a coat or a gown,
And a young lady with a Draper or Grocer may well sit down.
A Draper or Grocer for a young lady may have a good seat,
And to take home a young lady they need not be very far beat.
The young lady can either get a gown or a shawl,
A bonnie young laddie to come at e'en is surely best of all.
A Draper or Grocer's lady may very comfortable be,
When they come in at e'en*, they will get a comfortable cup of tea.
I hope the Grocers in their day some good will do, [evening]
Respectable Grocers in our country there's not a few.
Everyone must live by their own trade,
And to see all people comfortable I am very glad.
Happy may the Grocers and Drapers with their lovers be,
A great deal of their trade is among the sugar and tea.
As peace with China of late did proclaim,
I hope cheap sugar and tea we will get hame*. [home]
This peace in our country will likely raise the trade,
And of that many poor working person will be glad.
If working people work again should find,
To make good use of their money I hope they will be inclined,
If working people would but save one halfpenny each day,
They would see need for it when distress comes in their way.
To speak about the merchants I now do incline,
This little poem for them was my design.
I hope they will have servants at their demand,
And in kindness they will them command.
It's a very great sign of a Christian mind,
When masters and servants to each other are kind.
To one another every one of us should be just and true,
And at death none of us shall hape* that to rue. [hope]
If it be Drapers' and Grocers' fortune a family to have,
They will likely remind the young ones of the grave.
Set before children always a good example,
And if they live till they are old they will likely keep the sample.

Janet Reid, 1842.

Tune: *Johnny Cope* Jemmie Forrest

Chorus
Hey, Jemmie Forrest, are ye waukin'* yet? [waking]
Or are your Bailies* snoring yet? [Councillors]
If ye were waukin' I would wait,
Ye'd hae* a merry, merry morning. [have]

The frigate guns they loud did roar,
But louder did the Bailies snore,
And thought it was an unco* bore [extreme]
To rise up in the morning.

And syne* the Castle thunder'd loud; [then]
But kipper it is a savoury food,
And that the Bailies understood,
Sae early in the morning.

The Queen she's come to Granton Pier,
Nae Provost and nae Bailies here?
They're in their beds, I muckle* fear, [greatly]
Sae early in the morning.

The Queen she's come to Brandon Street,
The Provost and the Keys to meet,
And div* ye think that she's to wait [do]
Your waukin' in the morning.

My Lord, my Lord, the Queen she's here,
And vow, my Lord he lookit queer —
And what sets her sae* soon aster*? [so, astir]
It's barely nine in the morning.

Gae bring to me my robes o' state;
Come, Bailies, we will catch her yet.
Rin, rin*, my Lord, ye'll be o'er late, [Run, run]
She's been through town this morning.

Awa' to Dalkeith ye maun hie*, [must go]
To make your best apologie.
The Queen, she'll say, O fie! O fie!!
Ye're lazy loons in the morning.

[*Anonymous*]

A CHECK FOR SCOFFERS

Proverbs first, St Matthew seven and sixteen –
I always thought the scorner's chair was mean.
Psalms first, fiftieth, and ninety-fort –
And with sober people always resort.
Likewise Paraphrase ten, eleven, and fourteen,
And never take up your head with people that are mean.
Let every respectable person lay the case home to their sel'*, [selves]
See how they would like to be sung through all the country, and especially at Airthrey Well.
When once people wishes the rocks and the mountains on them to fall,
There will be no time to sing about "Jamie Forrest" at all.
This grieved me very sore,
When I heard those creditable names through the country did roar.
There need no person be in any doubt,
But the sound of the Last Trumpet will find them out.
Mockers' bands will be made strong,
But this scorners has never thought upon.
The Scriptures they do often say,
That evil speaking should be always put away.
For all that ministers and good men will say,
Scoffers is often found in our day.
I wish this country with this small unpolished poem for to treat,
That they may not rue their mockery when it is too late.
When once the mockers are hid in the grave,
I hope the rising generation will better behave.
For the off-scourings of the earth to make a mock of men in station,
To many a one it was a sore vexation.
But I hope the like of this will not be sung again,
For all the time of our young Queen's reign.
I hope you will excuse me for my humble line –
To hold down scorners it is my design.
I wish this poem to be put in every newspaper through the land,
That scorners may learn their Bible to understand.

Janet Reid, 1842.

[See further explanation overleaf]

THE use of "Jamie Forrest" with double inverted commas in Janet Reid's poem *A Check for Scoffers* in Janet's chapbook *Poems on Various Subjects* (1846) shows that she is objecting to the song *Jemmie Forrest* sung on the streets in September 1842 to mock Sir James Forrest, the Lord Provost (Lord Mayor) of Edinburgh. Two earlier broadsides have 'James Forrest' without inverted commas. Broadsides of *Jemmie Forest* with a woodcut of the Royal coach but without a printer's imprint are viewable online at *The Word on the Street* on the website of the National Library of Scotland.

When Queen Victoria arrived in Edinburgh on 1 September 1842, HMS *Royal George* moored later than expected in Granton Harbour, Leith, near Edinburgh at 1 am in the early morning. Queen Victoria and Prince Albert came ashore at 8 am. Sir James Forrest and the Bailies (City Councillors) were meant to present the Queen with the Keys to the City of Edinburgh – but they had waited in vain the previous day and were not warned of her early-morning arrival and were not there to greet her. The Queen's open coach was met by the Royal Company of Archers (a body of Scottish noblemen and gentlemen) who were mistaken for assassins and they were attacked by the Queen's bodyguard in a near fatal brawl – there had been two attempts to shoot the Queen in June 1840 and in May 1842 in London. Queen Victoria and Prince Albert drove through Edinburgh to Dalkeith Palace without stopping.

Prince Charles Edward Stuart (Bonnie Prince Charlie) defeated the forces of King George II led by General Sir John Cope at the Battle of Prestonpans (fought on the site of a coalfield east of Edinburgh) in an early-morning surprise attack by circling around them under cover of darkness and charging them from behind at 6 am on 21 September 1845. *Jemmie Forest* is a parody of *Hey, Johnny Cope, are ye waukin yet?* by Adam Skirving (1719-1803) on the defeat of the English forces. It was later rendered as *Sir John Cope Trode the North Right Far* by Robert Burns (1759-1796 with the chorus:

> Hey, Johnnie Cope, are ye wauking yet?
> Or are ye sleeping I would wait;
> O, haste ye get up, for the drums do beat;
> O fye! Cope, rise in the morning.
>
> *Robert Burns*

THE QUEEN'S FAREWELL

It was in the year Eighteen Hundred and Forty-Two,
Good people in Scotland this will surely please you now.
It was on the thirteenth day of September,
Which good people will likely long remember,
Her Majesty came through Dunblane and the Brig o' Allan,
Where many respectable people at present are dwallin'*. [dwelling]
But Brig o' Allan people would be in far better cheer,
If she had taken down the head of her carriage when she came here.
Her Majesty was better seen in Stirling I am told –
There she was admired by young and by old.
The cannons at Stirling Castle was firing,
And to see her Majesty all people had a desiring.
But now our young Queen and Prince Albert are gone home –
I wish God's blessing may be with them when they are gone.
And now for a time we must bid our young Queen farewell –
God's blessing on her and her subjects wherever they do dwell.
The King of Kings we should always desire to see –
Beauty in Him with believers will always be.
Our young Queen is mortal as well as oursel'*, [ourselves]
It is but a few years any of us on earth has to dwell.
Our pleasures on earth are as but for a day,
For time with every one of us is fast flying away.
We should always set our hearts beyond the grave,
Where through Christ's sufferings pleasures evermore we may have.
We should take a turn in our thoughts on Calvary every day,
And remember how our Saviour for our sins did bleed and pray.
We should mind how he was pierced in both hands and feet,
And to one another should always be discreet.
We should always mind Christ's golden rule,
And to one another should never be cruel.
Her Majesty and Prince Albert a part of Scotland has seen –
When they go home I hope they will remember the poor and the mean.
Through Christ's merits may God bless the Queen,
And likewise all her subjects both rich and mean.

Janet Reid, 1842.

FOR THE

NEW-YEAR.

This is now the year Eighteen Hundred and Forty-three,
There will be alterations in it, and that we will see.
There was two strange things happened in Scotland in the year
Forty-two,
It is well known by every one to be true,
Our young Queen to Scotland she did come,
To be sure it was very good news to some.
But likewise there has happened a sore-distressing case,
But our beloved ministers in their own churches we will not see
their face.
I hope the King of kings their friend will always be,
Altho' some of them may yet have to cross the sea.
I hope Elijah's God where'er they be will them feed.
Of God's care sure all of us do need.
For all them that trust in him will never lack their bread,
Altho' to our grief we may see other ministers in their stead;
We should all learn contented for to be,
For many is the alteration every year we see.
We should always mind what our Saviour to Mary did say,
We should all mind the one thing needful in our day.
Edinburgh and Glasgow will soon be filled up too,
With a generation that follows us they all will be new,
In a few short years we will all be dead and gone,
And even Queen Victoria herself must also leave the throne.
We should always set our hearts beyond the grave,
Both rich and poor should soberly behave.
We should mind what Joseph to his brethren did say,—
See that you do not fall out by the way,
To one another we should always be kind and true,
And at death none of us will ever have cause to rue.
We all know that Christ's blood cleanses from all sin
But for all this to sinful actions we should never run,
When we think on what the lines above do say,
We should always think upon our dying day.

JANET REID, Carnock, Fifeshire.

Gilchrist, Printer, Glasgow.

Peter Forbes' album. *Printed by William Gilchrist, Glasgow, 1843.*

FOR THE NEW-YEAR

This is now the year Eighteen Hundred and Forty-Three,
There will be alterations in it, and that we will see.
There was two strange things happened in Scotland in the year 'Forty-Two,
It is well known by everyone to be true.
Our young Queen to Scotland she did come,
To be sure it was very good news to some.
But likewise there happened a sore distressing case,
But our beloved ministers in their own churches we will not see their face.
I hope the King of Kings their friend will always be,
Altho' some of them may yet have to cross the sea.
I hope Elijah's God, where'er they be, will them feed,
Of God's care sure all of us do need.
For all them that trust in him will never lack their bread,
Altho' to our grief we may see other ministers in their stead;
We should all learn contented for to be,
For many is the alteration every year we see.
We should always mind what our Saviour to Mary did say,
We should all mind the one thing needful in our day.
Edinburgh and Glasgow will soon be filled up too,
With a generation that follows us they all will be new.
In a few short years we will all be dead and gone,
And even Queen Victoria herself must also leave the throne.
We should always set our hearts beyond the grave,
Both rich and poor should soberly behave.
We should mind what Joseph to his brethren did say –
See that you do not fall out by the way.
To one another we should always be kind and true,
And at death none of us will ever have cause to rue.
We all know that Christ's blood cleanses from all sin,
But for all this to sinful actions we should never run.
When we think on what the lines above do say,
We should always think upon our dying day.

Janet Reid, 1843.

ERSKINE BEVERIDGE (1853-1920) in *A Bibliography of Works Relating to Dunfermline and the West of Fife* (1901) records a broadside of the poem *On Peace in Every Church* by Janet Reid 'entered upon outside authority' which has not been found. Judging from its title, this poem was probably composed soon after the Disruption of the Church of Scotland on 18 May 1843.

The Church of Scotland (the Kirk) was established by the Scottish Parliament in 1592 after the Reformation of 1560. The Kirk claimed the right to independent jurisdiction of its own affairs by governing bodies of clergy and lay members. This was incorporated into the Act of Union of Scotland and England in 1707. However the right of patronage (which also existed in England) was restored in Scotland in 1712. This gave the owners of the kirks (the builders or their heirs – landowners, clan chiefs, town councils, universities or the Crown) the right to appoint church ministers in local parishes.

In the dispute over patronage the term 'intrusion' is used to mean the right of patrons to appoint ministers; and the term 'non-intrusion' is used to mean the right of the congregations to choose their own ministers. The Church of Scotland was divided into 'moderates' who accepted the right of patrons to appoint ministers; and 'evangelicals' who believed that congregations should have the final say. In 1834 the evangelicals persuaded the General Assembly of the Church to pass a 'Veto Act' which allowed a congregation to block a minister whom they did not want. This meant that church law contradicted secular law which led to protracted legal disputes.

In 1842 a 'Claim, Declaration and Protest, Anent [Concerning] the Encroachment of the Court of Session' was made against patronage. It was produced for the Church of Scotland by the Rev. Thomas Chalmers (1780-1847) the leader of the evangelicals. This appeal was rejected by Parliament in January 1843. Thomas Chalmers called for a 'disruption between church and state' at the General Assembly of the Church of Scotland in Edinburgh on 18 May 1843. He led one third of the clergy (471 out of the 1203 ministers present) to walk out in protest. They resigned their livings and lost their homes. They founded the Free Church of Scotland and built new churches and new manses from funds raised by the members of the congregations that followed them.

ON THE FAITHFUL MINISTERS OF THE CHURCH OF SCOTLAND

The Church of Scotland's ministers has gotten Mr Gillespie's spirit now,
I hope great good in their day they yet will do.
There's many a misty morning has turned out a bonny day,
I hope confusion in the Church will soon wear away –
For our beloved ministers will build Churches of Relief,
And amongst many others the Church of Scotland will be the chief.
To a good cause they have been both trusty and true,
And at death, I hope, none of them will ever have to rue.
We must all own this non-intrusion,
Has brought on the Church of Scotland a great confusion.
From many an eye, for them, has dropt many a tear,
But in God's strength of our good ministers, I hope there will be no fear.
We have all, and every one of us, the promise of bread and water,
But for all this, many a one gets a sore scatter*. [loss]
The Psalmist, David the King of Israel, he did say –
Ere ever he was afflicted, he went astray.
The seven ministers of Strathbogie,
Had surely hain* great love for a fu' coggie*. [saved,
They had hain more love for a fu' bowl, full wooden bowl]
Than they had for any person's soul.
They put that unbeloved minister in,
For the seven ministers of Strathbogie – it surely was a sin.
Auchterarder Presbytery was all as one,
And they have acted faithful to both woman and man.
Although Auchterarder Church long has vacant been,
I hope a godly minister will in it yet be seen.
For the beloved Church of Scotland many a one would part their last bawbee*, [halfpenny]
For there is justice in the ministers, and that we plainly see.
If I had money of my own for to spare,
Mr Gillespie's Old Church, for Carnock minister, I would repair.
Now, Church of Scotland's ministers, I bid you all adieu,
And I wish the blessings of God may be always with you.

Janet Reid, 1843.

ON RESPECTABLE BAKERS

Bakers! They do serve both rich and poor,
Carrying the bread from door to door.
People, to Bakers, should be very well *bred*,
For everyone must live by their own trade.
Bakers, unto the poor, are not very shy,
For they often give them a piece as they pass by.
Them that to the poor doth give, unto the Lord doth lend,
And in His own time and way, back will it send.
But, for all this, Bakers have their Merchants to pay,
And giving away a great deal, they must sometimes delay.
Likewise, they have their families to bring up,
And of Tea, they must have a bit cup.
Happy may them and their families be,
And always have a little the poor for to gi'e*; [give]
For our blessed Saviour unto us did say –
'The poor you will always have in your way'.
For some of the poor, their own enemies have been,
And that, at this day, is plainly seen.
If Bakers have good payment, they will likely have a good seat –
And none about them need want their meat.
Respectable people about Bakers do often go,
And I hope none of them will ever prove their foe.
Respectable people, the oven often need,
And they find it very handy indeed.
I hope better ways we yet will see,
And working people again, will get a fee!
If we, unto religion, would but turn,
For want of bread we would not need to mourn.

Janet Reid, 1843.

[See a broadside without a printer's imprint over the next leaf which is deduced as printed by Macdonald]

ON EDINBURGH CITY

Edinburgh is built near Arthur's Seat,
And to get fresh air folk cannot be beat;
The rail coaches between Edinburgh and Glasgow does run,
But I trust Sabbath running they soon will shun.
Each Sabbath in the church we all should meet,
If none of us or our dear friends be sick.
All they who for Heaven do intend,
I hope in God's service their lives on Earth will spend.
I think there are many of Edinburgh people sober and douse,
For I have seen the evidence of that in many a house.
There are many of them have the Samaritan nature,
For they appear to be kind to every creature.
In Edinburgh there's many a splendid shop,
And many a Christian there does stop.
For my uneven lines you will me excuse,
For the pen, that valuable thing, I was never learned to use.
Thanks be to the youths that my poems did write,
Although I sat by them and to them did dite*. [dictate]
Against me, some people has a clamour,
For in my little poems there is no grammar –
Such reek* as in the house must come out at the lum* – [smoke,
My little unpolished poems does please some. chimney]
Many a one cries out to me for fun,
But such things as Burns did write, by me shall ne'er be done.
Those that call for fun, comes to a dying day,
They'll see that religion can alone be their stay.
Edinburgh Castle on a rock doth stand,
I hope that the people of Edinburgh will never build on sand.
I trust the seventh chapter of St Matthew they will often see,
And they'll remember it, when they cannot see me.

Janet Reid, 1843. [See the broadside printed by Macdonald overleaf]

ON

RESPECTABLE BAKERS.

BAKERS! they do serve both rich and poor,
Carrying the bread from door to door.
People, to Bakers, should be very well *bred*,
For every one must live by their own trade.
Bakers, unto the poor, are not very shy,
For they often give them a piece as they pass by.
Them that to the poor doth give, unto the Lord doth lend,
And in His own time and way, back will it send.
But, for all this, Bakers have their Merchants to pay,
And giving away a great deal, they must sometimes delay.
Likewise, they have their families to bring up,
And of Tea, they must have a bit cup.
Happy may them and their families be,
And always have a little the poor for to gi'e;
For our blessed Saviour unto us did say—
"The poor you will always have in your way."
For some of the poor, their own enemies have been,
And that, at this day, is plainly seen.
If Bakers have good payment, they will likely have a good seat—
And none about them need want their meat.
Respectable people about Bakers do often go,
And I hope none of them will ever prove their foe.
Respectable people, the oven often need,
And they find it very handy indeed.
I hope better days we yet will see,
And working people again, will get a fee!
If we, unto religion, would but turn,
For want of bread we would not need to mourn.

JANET REID, CARNOCK, FIFESHIRE.

Peter Forbes' album. [*Printed by Macdonald, Edinburgh, 1843*]
[*See the poem on page 90*]

ON EDINBURGH CITY.

EDINBURGH is built near Arthur Seat,
And to get fresh air folk cannot be beat;
The rail coaches between Edinburgh and Glasgow does run,
But I trust Sabbath running they soon will shun.
Each Sabbath in the Church we all should meet,
If none of us or our dear friends be sick.
All they who for heaven do intend,
I hope in God's service their lives on earth will spend.
I think there are many of Edinburgh people sober and douse,
For I have seen the evidence of that in many a house;
There are many of them has the Samaritan nature,
For they appear to be kind to every creature.
In Edinburgh there many a splendid shop,
And many a Christian there does stop.
For my uneven lines you will me excuse,
For the pen, that valuable thing, I was never learned to use.
Thanks be to the youths that my poems did write,
Although I sat by them and to them did dite.
Against me, some people has a clamour,
For, in my little poems, there is no grammar.
Such reek as in the house must come out at the lum,
My little unpolished poems does please some.
Many a one cries out to me for fun,
But such things as Burns did write, by me ne'er shall be done.
Those that call for fun, comes to a dying day,
They'll see that religion can alone be their stay.
Edinburgh Castle on a rock doth stand,
I hope that the people of Edinburgh will never build on sand.
I trust the Seventh Chapter of Matthew they will often see,
And they'll remember it when they cannot see me.

JANET REID, CARNOCK, FIFESHIRE.

Macdonald, Printer, Carrubbers' Close, Edinburgh.

Peter Forbes' album. *Printed by Macdonald, Edinburgh, 1843.*
[*See the poem on page 91*]

DAVID LOVE (1750-1826), a 'chapman' or travelling pedlar of his own chapbooks and poems, may have had an influence on Janet Reid. His *A New and Correct Set of Godly Poems* has the imprint 'Culross, 1782'. Culross lies on the Firth of Forth, 4 miles south-west of Carnock and this was probably his mother's home. David Love writes in *Original Poems on Various Subjects* (1791):

> Most of these poems I composed in my youth [...]. They have been printed six times and generally approved by the commonality. Yet I am well assured there are many grammatical errors therein, but I cannot mend them. As I got only eleven months at School, I was not taught Grammar. If I have any gift in poetry, I received it from Nature. Whatever is defective by misplaced words or unpolished verse, I humbly hope the learned will not censure.

In *Life, Adventures, and Experiences of David Love, written by himself* (1824) he recounts travelling on foot around Scotland and then England composing poems and selling chapbooks printed on route. He married once in Scotland and twice in Nottingham (marrying his third wife who was 29 years younger in 1810) and had eleven children in all. He finally settled in Nottingham in 1816.

Perhaps David Love visited Carnock Fair before he left Scotland in 1782 though Janet Reid was probably too young to encounter him there. He tells how on reaching a fair he 'got a stool, mounted and thus began my harangue':

> Good people, here are two excellent new songs never before printed, composed by myself, your humble servant. One is *The Pride and Vanity of Young Women, with advice to Young Men that they may take good care who they marry*. And that the young women may not be offended, I have another which may serve as an answer, *The Pride and Vanity of Young Men, with advice to the Maids, to beware of being ensnared by their flatteries, and enticing words*. I soon drew hundreds about me, where I boldly stood, and there I sang aloud, before a gaping crowd. I sold all my songs the first day of the fair, and was sorry I did not bring two thousand more songs with me [...] the men buying the songs concerning the women, and the women that of the men.
>
> *David Love*

BE MERCIFUL TO BODY AND TO BEAST

There is very little mercy in our land,
For the poor horses are abused on every hand.
There were six-and-twenty sinners came in a wanded creel –
They had very much the appearance as if driving to the de'il*. [devil]
To the poor horses it surely was no fun –
When with cruel sinners they had so fast to run.
When the lumps of froth fell from each horse's side –
They surely had too fast to ride.
Thirteen cruel sinners for every horse –
The case could not be very much worse.
No mercy to the poor horses is ever shown –
But hereafter about that it may yet be known.
A horse is a very useful beast –
But many a one to abuse them make their jest.
The poor of the land are now in starvation,
And the poor horses are abused by people in every station.
The carters are as bad as any of them a'*, [all]
For with cruelty they often do the poor horses ca'*. [cut]
But the time is fast hastening on,
When the poor horses out of their slavery will be gone.
When Balaam's ass got the power to speak,
It complained of its master, who did it beat.
God's mercies man does often abuse,
And the poor horses are often ill-used.
Horse drivers, read the second chapter of St James,
And be kind to horses when ye tie them in their hames*. [homes]
A horse is a very useful beast in our land,
But it is abused on every side, as we do understand.
Horses are ill-used by both rich and poor,
And of that we are all very sure.
You should try your poor horses better to use,
In case in some unexpected hour you get a bruise.

Janet Reid, 1843.

ON THE LOSS OF THE PEGASUS STEAMER

In July, Eighteen Hundred and Forty-Three,
This steamer sunk in the deep, deep sea;
Leaving many a one with hearts full sore,
For friends they never will see more;
And many now are left to mourn,
For friends that never can return.
They in a watery grave do sleep,
While many a friend for them does weep.
The mercy sought, I hope, was found,
Which should comfort those whose friends are drowned.
There's a time to be born and a time to die,
And that time no one can pass by.
The Rev. Mr McKenzie was amongst the rest,
And he the Saviour solemnly addressed.
He raised a prayer to heaven's throne,
That mercy to them might be shown.
I hope his prayers would be heard,
When he sincerely spoke the word.
It was sad news when it came to shore,
That many friends were now no more.
But I hope they'll meet on another day,
When sea and land have passed away.
I trust they'll meet on that happy shore,
Where sin and sorrow are known no more.
Our time in life is all but short,
So to religion we always should resort;
And always good company should keep,
For we know not but our grave may be in the deep.
People say they should have gone round the rock,
But the sailors, I suppose, were all skilled folk;
For many had passed that way before –
But days in this world these had no more.
I'm sorry for the friends who are left behind,
But I hope in God's Word they'll consolation find.
We're told in the Word we ought not to weep,
When friends in Jesus fall asleep.

Janet Reid, 1843. [See the broadside on page 150]

ON VAN AMBURGH'S EXHIBITION AT BRIDGE OF ALLAN

In the year 'Forty-Three, on the eighth of September,
Good people will likely it long remember,
That it was a beautiful sunshine day,
When Van Amburgh and his Company came this way.
Some of the horses were grey, and others the colour of cream –
Many of the strangers never saw the like at their ain hame*. [own
Such a bonny sight was never at the Brig o' Allan before, home]
Since they for lodgers did keep an open door.
In Mr Barr's Park they pitched their tent,
To see the strange sight many ladies and gentlemen went.
Many a curious sight there we did see,
But the puggy* riding on the pony best pleased me. [doggy]
The elephant's back was very wide –
With pleasure upon it children did ride.
At the bonny spotted giraffe,
At its long neck, many a one did laugh.
Van Amburgh beside the lion and leopard did go in,
And the lion with him made a very little din.
On the leopard's skin were many a pretty spot,
And round its cage it did often trot.
A black tiger is a great wonder for to see,
Many a respectable person told me.
A little boy tried to ride upon the bonny horse,
But he soon found himself at a great loss.
The puggy by far did him beat,
For he always kept upon his seat.
Success to Van Amburgh and his Company where'er they go;
I hope no one to them will ever prove a foe.
On September the ninth day,
Van Amburgh and his pretty carriages went respectably away;
And, along with him, his cheerful band –
The like of Van Amburgh and his Company is not in all the land.
It was a pretty sight to see a gentleman's eight cream-coloured
horses for to drive –
I hope in our land they will always prosper and thrive.

Janet Reid, 1843.

ON THE YEAR 1844.

THIS is now the year fourty-four,
And all contentions should be given o'er;
We should live like sister and like brother—
And none should be vicious against one another.
We should a' be friendly to ane anither in our short day,
For time wi' every one of us, is flying fast away.
Mind! what Jóseph to his brethren did say—
" See that ye fall not out by the way."
Remember Joshua, who was aye sober and douce,
Let every one remember themselves, or their ain house.
The 25th chapter of Matthew often read,
And follow it in many a deed.
Read the 13th chapter of St. John,
And our Saviour's humility often think upon.
He gave us there a commandment that was new,
That to ane anither we should always be just and true.
It is said in Scripture, how beautiful are the Preacher's feet—
To each other of every *principle* we should be discreet.
Think of Christ's sufferings in the Garden and on the Tree,
How he suffered for sinners, such as you and me!
It's not fit to see among Christians so much separation—
The like of it should not be in a Christian nation.
The matter in our land is fairly settled now,
And every one with their own party should only have to do.
The country has lang been in a great confusion,
And all about this non-intrusion.
In heaven there will no disturbance be,
For our Bible tells us, in that holy place we must all agree.
I hope, through Jesus Christ, people will preach Salvation;
And that is a Gospel will suit every nation.
Read the 1st chapter of Second Peter,
And I hope you will excuse me for my old metre;
It is now ended the year forty-three,
And I hope people in Scotland will better agree.

JANET REID, BRIDGE OF ALLAN.

Peter Forbes' album. *[Printed by Macdonald, Edinburgh] 1844.*

ON THE YEAR 1844

This is now the year 'Forty-Four,
And all contentions should be given o'er;
We should live like sister and like brother –
And none should be vicious against one another.
We should a' be friendly to ane anither in our short day,
For time wi'* every one of us, is flying fast away. [with]
Mind! What Joseph to his brethren did say –
'See that ye fall not out by the way.'
Remember Joshua, who was aye* sober and douce, [ever]
Let everyone remember themselves, or their ain* house. [own]
The twenty-fifth chapter of St Matthew often read,
And follow it in many a deed.
Read the thirteenth chapter of St John,
And our Saviour's humility often think upon.
He gave us there a commandment that was knew,
That to ane anither we should always be just and true.
It is said in Scripture, how beautiful are the Preacher's feet –
To each other of every principle we should be discreet.
Think of Christ's sufferings in the Garden and on the Tree*, [Cross]
How he suffered for sinners, such as you and me!
It's not fit to see among Christians so much separation –
The like of it should not be in a Christian nation.
The matter in our land is fairly settled now,
And everyone with their own party should only have to do.
The country has lang* been in a great confusion, [long]
And all about this non-intrusion.
In heaven there will no disturbance be,
For our Bible tells us, in that holy place we must all agree.
I hope, through Jesus Christ, people will preach Salvation;
And that is a Gospel will suit every nation.
Read the first chapter of Second Peter,
And I hope you will excuse me for my old metre;
It is now ended the year 'Forty-Three,
And I hope people in Scotland will better agree.

Janet Reid, 1844.

ON THE DISTRESS OF THE

WORKING CLASSES.

When working people work they cannot get,
Sure them and their families must solitary sit.
Many a one, for such starvation,
Is forced to leave the Scottish nation.
Hardships there they must also see,
Besides the danger in crossing the raging sea.
Likewise removing from father and mother,
Few friends there to comfort one another.
I think if people could rightly the matter understand,
There is plenty to maintain every person in the land.
I hope the rich will the poor's case consider,
For few workers at this time can help sister or brother.
Many a one says the cause is owing to drink;
But many come to poverty without that, I think.
O! what the want of work will do,
It is known to all the country to be true.
I am very sorry for the people at my ain hame,
And to feel for them I cannot be to blame.
For Dumfermline and Carnock I grieve very sore;
Perhaps some of them I never may see more.
But I hope trade will revive again in the West Nook o' Fife,
Where I did spend the most part of my life.
Now I have taken a habitation in the west countrie,
And the people there is very kind to me.
I may thank God, though far from my home,
To my fellow-creature I never need to make moan.
The people is always very kind to me;
I never want a comfortable cup of tea.
There is many a misty morning turns out a bonny day;
I hope dull trade from the country will soon wear away.
Good people, read the third chapter of Saint Luke,
You will see good counsel in that holy book.
Remember what John the Baptist did say—
Them that has both meat and clothes to give part away.

JANET REID, *Bridge of Allan*

Gilchrist, Printer, 145 Argyle Street.

Peter Forbes' album. *Printed by William Gilchrist, Glasgow, 1844.*

ON THE DISTRESS OF THE WORKING CLASSES

When working people work they cannot get,
Sure them and their families must solitary sit.
Many a one, for such starvation,
Is forced to leave the Scottish nation.
Hardships there they must also see,
Besides the danger in crossing the raging sea.
Likewise removing from father and mother,
Few friends there to comfort one another.
I think if people could rightly the matter understand,
There is plenty to maintain every person in the land.
I hope the rich will the poor's case consider,
For few workers at this time can help sister or brother.
Many a one says the cause is owing to drink;
But many come to poverty without that, I think.
O! what the want of work will do,
It is known to all the country to be true.
I am very sorry for the people at my ain hame*, [own home]
And to feel for them I cannot be to blame.
For Dunfermline and Carnock I grieve very sore;
Perhaps some of them I never may see more.
But I hope trade may revive again in the West Nook* o' Fife,
Where I did spend the most part of my life. [Corner]
Now I have taken a habitation in the west countrie,
And the people there is very kind to me,
I may thank God, though far from my home,
To my fellow-creature I never need to make moan.
The people is always very kind to me;
I never want a comfortable cup of tea.
There is many a misty morning turns out a bonny day;
I hope dull trade from the country will soon wear away.
Good people, read the third chapter of Saint Luke,
You will see good counsel in that Holy Book.
Remember what John the Baptist did say –
Them that has both meat and clothes, to give part away.

Janet Reid, 1844.

ON AN UNFORTUNATE LADY

No lady should give a man her hand,
If she does not love him, we may understand.
No parents into marriage should take part,
In case afterwards the parties come to smart.
A lady, against her mind, should never give herself away,
For there is danger afterwards, and that we may say.
Both men and women should marry their heart's desire
And of one another they are not likely for to tire.
They will never offer each other a pickle of the white*, [little of the
And in each other's company they will often take delight. wheat]
Far better to go about with the rake and the howe*, [hoe]
For love in the first Garden in it did grow.
I wish this may be a warning to parents in every place,
That they may never bring their children to disgrace.
Although from the bar of man she has won free,
She'll remember, over her, there's an all-seeing ee*. [eye]
I hope in bitterness she will lament,
And, through God's grace, she will truly repent –
Christ came the chief of sinners for to save,
I hope afterwards this will be a warning to all to behave.
If she be innocent, it's a pity to bring her to disgrace;
I'm sorry such tidings should be told in our own place.
There's neither man nor woman has life in their own hand,
Parents over children in marriage should have no command.
True, love in this land has ruined many;
But, by right, it should never ruin any.
Although marriage is only for this life,
True love makes a happy husband and wife.
In this misfortune, the parents, some say, are to blame,
For they should have let the poor lady stop at hame;
Or else married another man for her joe*, [sweetheart]
And to him she would never likely prov'd a foe.

Janet Reid, 1844.

ON THE READING-ROOM

The Reading-Room is an eight-cornered house,
And the people that belong to it appear to be both sober and douce.
The Reading-Room before the Bowling-Green does stand,
And on the sign there is the shape of a hand.
It is a pretty sign that hangs before the door –
In all my travels I never saw the like of it before.
There is the sign of violets just as they grow, [cornflowers, fade]
And likewise the sign of bachelor buttons* that never do dow*.
And there is likewise the sign of love-lies-bleeding*, [red cockscomb]
And I hope of that young lovers will not be needing.
And likewise there is a flower of colour blue,
And I hope young lovers to each other will always be true.
And there is many a picture within around the wall,
And many respectable people give the Reading-Room a call.
There are newspapers there, as we do understand,
To tell them the news from every land.
There is a Library always ready,
With books to please either gentleman or lady.
A bonny clock on the stair head does stand,
And they will see the time of day just at their hand.
Although this clock has not a music bell,
Yet the time of day she does pointedly tell.
Major Henderson has now come hame*, [home]
And to visit his bonny houses he cannot be to blame.
Major Henderson has made a pretty walk to the Bowling-Green,
Few like it in the country is to be seen.
I hope Major Henderson will grow in grace,
And be an honour to all his friends in his own place.
Major Henderson was once far awa'*, [away]
And I wish health and prosperity may always on him fa'*. [fall]
Major Henderson is Laird of Westertown too,
And much good about the Brig o' Allan he does do.
He has made in Brig o' Allan a bonny Bowling-Green,
Which is most pleasant to be seen.

Janet Reid, 1844.

ON THE BONNY NEW CHURCH
AT THE BRIDGE OF ALLAN

This Church was built in the year Eighteen Hundred and
    Forty-Three –
It's a bonny Church without and within we may see.
Although it is a Church without a steeple,
I hope about it there will always be a righteous people.
A new generation in a few short years soon will arise,
And I hope one another they will never despise;
It is not fit to see among Christians so much separation,
The like of it should not be in a Christian nation.
Good people read Christ's Sermon on the Mount,
And in every one of your actions at it point;
Read the fourteenth and fifteenth chapters of St John,
And the tenth of Hebrews often think upon;
Read the eighty-and-fourth Psalm,
And to one another be always kind and calm.
We should all live like sister and like brother,
And none should be vicious against one another.
We should always look down to our own black feet,
And about our neighbours' faults never leet*. [list]
Mind what our Saviour to the people did say,
Them that is without sin let them cast the first stone away.
Mind what Joseph to his brethren did say –
'See that ye fall not out by the way.'
We are all but in the wilderness, and on the road,
But in a few short years we will all be in our fixed abode;
We must all leave our little Church to others to possess –
The Bridge of Allan people will be kind to people in distress.
In Bridge of Allan there will soon rise a new generation,
I wish they may never bring on themselves or their minister vexation.
It is said in Scripture, how beautiful are the preacher's feet,
To one another in every principle we should be discreet.
I saw the first stone of this little Church laid down –
I hope people, after this, will never on each other frown.
Good people read your Testaments Old and New,
And they will teach old and young how to do.

Janet Reid, 1844.

ON THE OPENING OF THE NEW SCHOOL AT BRIDGE OF ALLAN

I think good people will likely long remember,
In Eighteen Forty-Four, the fourth day of November,
This School was opened with God's praise,
And the young ones in the school sweet notes did raise.
The thirty-third verse of the hundred and nineteenth Psalm,
And I hope the scholars to each other will always be kind and calm.
I hope they will go quietly out of the School,
And through God's strength on the road will never act the fool.
I hope them and their parents will thank God every day,
That ever He sent such a good teacher this way.
Three ministers were present, and they did all agree,
That he was the best teacher that ever they did see.
He walked about that night with a white wand,
And the children he did mildly command.
They readily obeyed him in every word,
As if he had stood over them with a drawn sword.
I hope it will be known at a future day,
That he was leading them in the true heavenly way.
Now, with preacher and teacher, Bridge of Allan is truly blest,
But on Christ's finished work for salvation we alone must trust.
A good preacher and teacher are helps to human nature,
For everyone well knows that he is a fallen creature.
The opening of the School was a happy night at Bridge of Allan,
Many respectable persons came a good way from their own dwallin'.
A comfortable cup of tea there we all did get,
And with pleasure there all the company did sit.
Our beloved minister at the head of the company did stand,
To honour them, with his cup and flat* in his hand. [saucer]
But by all the company that learning had,
To hear the teacher well approved of, I was very glad.
The worthy Major got cheers three,
And with that the company did all agree.
Thanks to God we have got the Major back again,
And long amongst us may he remain.
Our worthy old minister thought it was very right,
To thank Mr McRobie and likewise Mr Wright.

Janet Reid, 1844.

Milsey Bank Female School.

THIS School was visited by four ministers that day,
And much good of the teacher the gentlemen had to say.
The worthy gentleman in Keir presents did them send;
He wishes them much of their youth in religion to spend.
He has long been a worthy gentleman about this place;
He wishes both old and young daily to grow in grace.
I think each of them on their presents should put his name,
Or else they surely will be to blame,
That the children may have his worthy name to read
After he is numbered among the dead.
The ministers gave the children all a good advice,
To learn in their young years for to be wise.
They told them both evening and morning for to pray—
For time with them, both old and young, is flying fast away.
They all agreed that the teacher was leading them wisely on,
And the children to these gentlemen did sing a heavenly song.
I hope they will often see what is within their Bible,
And in searching the Scriptures they will not be idle.
The children of Israel's wanderings there they will see—
And away from every idol I hope they will flee.
Be sure to fly from the dangers of the Church of Rome,
For that by every one should be done.
There is too much evil in our nation;
But by the Church of Rome we need not be brought into vexation.
But their worthy teacher will them direct;
And the young ones for her will always have respect.
I think it a very good thing to teach them in a school by their lone,
That the big ones would not abuse them on their road going home.
The little children have always good will to go to school;
Their teacher will teach them on the road never to act the fool.
I hope she and her scholars will hereafter each other see,
Where sun nor moon will never need to be.

JANET REID, BRIDGE OF ALLAN.

PRINTED IN THE STIRLING OBSERVER OFFICE.

Peter Forbes' album. *Printed in the Stirling Observer Office, 1844.*

MILSEY BANK FEMALE SCHOOL

This School was visited by four ministers that day,
And much good of the teacher the gentlemen had to say.
The worthy gentleman in Keir presents did them send;
He wishes them much of their youth in religion to spend.
He has long been a worthy gentleman about this place;
He wishes both old and young daily to grow in grace.
I think each of them on their presents should put his name,
Or else they surely will be to blame,
That the children may have his worthy name to read
After he is numbered among the dead.
The ministers gave the children all a good advice,
To learn in their young years for to be wise.
They told them both evening and morning for to pray –
For time with them, both young and old, is flying fast away.
They all agreed that the teacher was leading them wisely on,
And the children to these gentlemen did sing a heavenly song.
I hope they will often see what is within their Bible,
And in searching the Scriptures they will not be idle.
The children of Israel's wanderings there they will see –
And away from every idol, I hope they will flee.
Be sure to fly from the dangers of the Church of Rome,
For that by everyone should be done.
There is too much evil in our nation;
But by the Church of Rome we need not be brought into vexation.
But their worthy teacher will them direct;
And the young ones for her will always have respect.
I think it is a very good thing to teach them in a school by their lone,
That the big ones would not abuse them on their road going home.
The little children have always good will to go to school;
Their teacher will teach them on the road never to act the fool.
I hope she and her scholars will hereafter each other see,
Where sun nor moon will never need to be.

Janet Reid, 1844.

ON THE FARMERS

For the Farmers I hae always had great respect –
For my welfare in former years they did not neglect.
O may their fields with wheat, corn, and barley be clad,
For to hear of their welfare I've always been glad.
O well may the good Farmers' tatties* and turnips grow, [potatoes]
And I hope they will not howk* them until the shaws do dow*. [dig, stalks do wilt]
I hope they'll have plenty of sweet milk and meal,
For that in our country is a very good tale.
And I hope each of them will have a good wife,
To keep them comfortable a' the days o' their life.
I'd advise the young Farmer that has not a lady,
That he should take one home as soon as he's ready.
And I doubt not he'll be to his wife very kind,
And keep her welfare oftentimes in his mind.
And she in return will be likely the same,
And long both together I wish they may remain.
And when in autumn their crops they get in,
I wish it may be wholesome and very well won.
I hope they remember whence their mercies do flow,
That it is neither from him that does till or sow.
Yet it's needful that they should the ground improve,
Else they need not expect the blessing from above.
When man was first made, he was not to be idle,
So when Farmers mind their farms, they should also mind their Bible.
I hope you'll give your children a good education,
To fit them to pass through the world in any station.
At all times show to children a virtuous example,
So that when they grow old they may follow the sample.
The Farmers will have good sons and fair daughters too,
And I trust in their day much good they may do.
Now good honest Farmers, both here and far awa'*, [away]
I wish bright prosperity may aye* on you fa'*. [ever, fall]
To wish the Farmers well I cannot be to blame,
For they were very kind to me at my ain dear hame.

Janet Reid, 1845.

ON THE GARDENERS

A Gardener surely has a pleasant trade –
If I had been a man, to be a Gardener I would have been very glad.
Within the walls of the garden grows many a pretty flower;
And they're always growing and decaying we are very sure.
They resemble in this both woman and man,
But the Gardener will dress them up as well as he can.
In the garden there grows both rue and thyme,
And to pu'* them together young people will incline. [pull]
There grows there a flower called love-lies-bleeding
Of that I hope my young lovers will not be needing.
But they will pull the bonny lily,
For to hing their heads like that other flower they'll not be so silly;
Up very soon will start another,
They'll love them better than either sister or brother.
In every month you'll see a flower fresh and young,
And people with one another must always have fun.
And apples in the garden they likewise do grow,
But, like man and woman, they through time to dow*. [fade]
Young people through time their hair grows grey,
And they should remember their time of youth fast wears away.
I would wish young people always to remember,
That there's many a pretty youth never sees December.
Although on earth they should have a short time,
I trust that to righteousness they'll always incline.
Now, as with the Gardeners I did begin,
They'll mind t'was in a garden woman and man first did sin.
We are indeed of the female sex,
And to mind our own frailty we should not neglect.
Many a one wishes to praise aye* themsel'; [ever]
But in this they do not do well.
The seventh chapter of St Matthew you will read,
And you should not wink at your own evil deed.

Janet Reid, 1845.

ON THE SHOEMAKERS

[1] Although we should have ever so many braw* clothes, [fine]
[2] Without shoes we would hae very cold toes.
[7] Although we should have braw shoes, we should not have pride,
[8] For they first grew upon the cows' and horses' side.
[9] It must be steeped amongst the bark that grows upon the tree,
[10] Ere ever it can be answerable for either you or me.
[13] If leather shoes Ladies do not please,
[14] The Shoemakers can make them of the cloth that makes the claes*. [clothes]
[15] But for all this, they must be firm with leather below –
[16] Or to the street, the finest Lady could not go.
[23] I trust Shoemakers will be men that are devout –
[24] I trust they'll never wear the drunkard's coat.
[25] Shoemakers will likely have good plans,
[26] And set a good example before young ones.
[27] Young people's minds are ready to be full of vanity,
[28] But the youngest and gayest death cannot defy.
Mind what King Solomon the preacher did say,
When he drew near the end of his day.
To be sure Shoemakers have a wearisome seat,
But with wind and rain they cannot be beat.
Although some be rich, and others be poor,
He said 'all is vanity', and that we are sure.
A Shoemaker should take home a wife and be content,
For our days on earth will soon all be spent.
I wish to give people all a good advice,
To learn in health and prosperity to be wise.
To one another we should be always just and true,
And at death, that is what we'll never rue.
Shoemaking is not a very wholesome trade,
But yet to be a Shoemaker many a one is glad.
Working people, by the sweat of their brow, must win their bread,
And there will be [no] Shoemakers and Tailors when we are dead.
Man at first was made of dust,
And unto that man and woman return they must.

Janet Reid, 1845.

[The first 16 lines are those numbered in *On the Gallant Shoemakers* on page 52]

ON THE JOLLY TAILORS

It is a long time since the Tailor trade began –
It was acted by the very first man;
But where they got their needles and their thread,
Concerning that we never yet did read.
It's a long time since the first sewsters returned to dust again,
But while the world stands Tailors must remain.
The weavers they do make their cloth both long and braid*, [broad]
But it can fit no man until it come to the Tailor trade.
The Tailors with their shears they do it shape,
And after that they sew it both firm and neat.
After the Tailor's hands, handsome looking it does remain,
Until that it returns to old rags again.
If at any time there be an alteration in the trade,
The Tailors they can make the coat-tails braid.
The Tailors with their lay-board and their goose*, [pressing-iron]
In this generation they are for very much use.
When I was young, a boy of me did take great care,
And learned me to read when he had time to spare;
When he grew up he became a Tailor about the place,
He never did himself or his friends disgrace;
He was always a man of good respect,
His lawful calling he never did neglect.
Success I wish unto all the sewing race,
I wish that they may daily grow in grace.
We should all learn contented for to be,
For many is the alteration every year we see.
For it is always by the Tailor trade
That rich and poor are neatly clad.

Janet Reid, 1845.

WILLIAM CAMERON (1785-1851), known as 'Hawkie', was probably encountered by Janet Reid when she visited Glasgow. He wrote *Hawkie: The Autobiography of a Gangrel* [Vagrant] in the Glasgow Work House during the winters of 1840-50. His manuscript was deciphered by Robert Donaldson, edited by John Strathesk and published in 1888 by David Robertson, a Glasgow bookseller:

> To those who knew Scotland well, especially Glasgow and the West during the first half of this century, the following pages will vividly recall the old, thin, lame, dust-begrimmed, poorly-clad figure of William Cameron, alias 'Hawkie', Beggar, Street Orator, and Wit. For, despite his inveterate love of a 'dram' and his furnishing in other respects a living illustration of Burns' line: 'Nae farther we can fa', his biting sarcasm, reckless wit and snell [fresh] 'hits' made him a general favourite.

'Hawkie' was born near Stirling, he was lamed as a child and he either 'cadged' (begged) or sold broadsides. He writes:

> I then went to Dunfermline; this is a good and charitable town. [...] I had been travelling all day, and was feeling tired: a gentleman passed me, and gave me a shilling; after going on a little he turned and gave me two and six pence. When I reached the end of Dunfermline I thought I could do no less than drink the giver's 'health'. I went into a public house and did so, but, finding the drouth [thirst] continue, I went into another and repeated the dose. When I got to the lodgings I unharnessed myself and went to a bookseller's named Miller for ballads or histories but he had nothing but [religious] tracts. These were a *bad fit*, but the drink being in the 'garret' I took four dozen of them, went into the street, and began a long story. I soon gathered an audience who relished the story and many bought. One of the buyers spurned his bargain and challenged me for an imposter, saying I had given him 'John Covey' in place of what I was calling. He demanded his halfpenny back, which I declined to do, and the crowd advised me to keep it. He went and told the town-keeper who came and took me to the black hole. As soon as the town-keeper was off, whisky was handed in through the stanchions. I was drunk all the time I was in 'quod' [jail], and, on Monday morning the town-keeper released me and ordered me out of the town.

ON THE FLESHERS

The Fleshers* keep their shops both clean and neat, [Butchers]
And butcher-meat to rich and poor it is a treat.
If the beasts the Fleshers could not fell,
Sure enough the meat they could not sell.
Fleshers can take out what they cannot put in,
And as soon as they get the life taken they begin to skin.
Every one of us may understand
That the Fleshers in their trade get many a bloody hand.
Fleshers in their trade get a great deal of toil,
But they can cut out a piece that will either roast or boil.
But they can cut out a piece which will answer any bride,
And then they can go about with their steel at their side.
They can cut it down and put it in a pie,
The bakers they can cover it and in the oven fry.
The richest nobles in all the land,
They all use butcher-meat, as we do understand.
As a good diet of it they can make,
I hope they will give their crumbs to the poor, and that is no mistake.
Many a one their dogs with butcher-meat do feed,
But none knows what they may come to need.
There is sometimes much between the cradle and the grave,
And people should always in a charitable manner behave.
Read the sixteenth chapter of St Luke,
And you will see how the rich man got his rebuke.
There is a great difference between the rich and the poor here,
But there was a greater difference in the parable, it does appear.
We should believe every word that our Saviour did say,
But many a one from his directions keep far away.
If everyone would help another,
The Fleshers may be able to help a poor sister or brother.
There are many poor persons in the land –
The rich the poor's case should understand,
For there are many, many poor in the land.

Janet Reid, 1845.

AGAINST SABBATH BREAKING

None was ever enriched by Sabbath gain –
None, thro' God's strength, should ever the Sabbath profane,
The Ten Commandments are all yet in force,
And none should break the Fourth to make the country worse.
When any person comes to ask horses on Sabbath day,
The master's answer should ever be, "Nay, nay, nay."
And they should say, "My poor horses must have rest,
"And my servants for the church they must be drest.
"My servants on Sabbath-day must go to church,
"And neither handle whip nor switch."
When I see people on Sabbath drive away,
I think they will rue that some other day.
They remind me of hounds hunting a tod* – [fox]
They sure enough go off the right road.
There are six working days in every week –
They will surely rue Sabbath visiting when they are sick;
Especially when they come to a dying hour,
Their Sabbath visits to The Trossachs will add no pleasure I'm sure.
Our Saviour's travels from heaven to earth should aye be in our
mind,
And to meditate on His sufferings all should be inclined.
Read Paraphrase forty-eight,
And in God's strength do all thing right.
Now I have little more to say —
Be sure your horses bear no burden on the Sabbath-day.
Them that keep horses read Psalm fifty —
To win money on Sabbath-day, see that you never be so thrifty.
And likewise them that ask horses away,
Remember there is a Judgement Day.
Read the fifty-eighth chapter of Isaiah,
And likewise the seventeenth of Jeremiah.
It has been a grief to me these many a Sabbath-day,
When I saw to the Trossachs sinners driving away.
Two horses I saw, on our sacramental day,
Mounted with a servant to go away —
To me it was a very sore grief,
But I could not give the servant relief.

That God in His own good time would alter the case,
We all have need for them to plead at a Throne of Grace,
For this world and its riches we must all leave behind,
I hope the master's and servant's eyes will not always be blind.

Janet Reid, 1845.

Six old woodcuts of women broadside-sellers.

ON A DAY OF HUMILIATION

I think there should be days of humiliation through all the nation,
For by the appearance of judgement we should be in vexation*.
We read in Old Testament time, [sorrow]
That to righteousness we should all incline.
For no doubt it is sin that makes us all to mourn,
For unto righteousness man and woman should return.
People should mind from whom all their mercies flow,
And in transgressors' ways we should never go.
There are both cruelty and pride –
Both by man and woman they should be laid aside.
There are both horse whipping and evil speaking;
About our neighbours' faults we should never be leeting*. [listing]
If people would take more notice of them that are poor,
It would be better than horse whipping, I am sure.
If they would let the poor horses stand longer in a stable,
I am sure to help the poor they would be able.
Good people, your talents never in a napkin tie,
Nor to the poor you never should prove shy.
The twenty-fifth chapter of St Matthew read –
I hope righteous people will follow it in every deed.
I hope the latter end of that chapter you will often see,
And everyone may think for himself how he may be.
Read the fourteenth and fifteenth chapters of St John,
And the first chapter of Proverbs often think upon.
Now, good people, I have little more to say –
Mind the poor and keep Holy the Sabbath-day.
There are not many Dorcases now in our day –
Our Dorcases are fallen sore away.
Cornelius's alms, as well as his prayers, did come
Before the Lord for a memorial of him.

Janet Reid, 1845.

ON THE SEVENTH OF NOVEMBER
or ON THE LOSS OF THE POTATOES

It is now drawing near the end of the year Eighteen Hundred and
Forty-Five,
Which many a one will remember while they are alive.
It was on that very same year the potatoes gave way –
I never saw nor heard of the like before in my day.
It certainly must be owing to sin;
But with my own corrupt nature I must first begin.
People should always begin at hame*, [home]
Before their neighbours they do blame.
We daily do see that fallen nature
Abounding always in every creature.
Everyone has their besetting sin;
But, I think, with everyone pride is taken in.
I think with greed many a one would cheat their brother,
And them that does that, will neither honour father nor mother.
The fourth commandment appears never to be seen,
Neither by the rich nor yet by the mean.
Humility is an ornament to everyone,
But it is seldom seen in either woman or man.
But many of them are fine at handling the whip,
And likewise at tumbling up the whisky and brandy cup.
There are many of the ladies not a whit better –
They would need 'Humility'* sent them in a letter. [*On Humility*]
The third chapter of Isaiah you will all read,
And remember that God Almighty sees every deed.
Pride surely must have a fa'*, [fall]
And for that at this time we are all appearing to get a ca'*. [call]
It is a sore affliction the cleanness of teeth;
It is God alone can give his people relief.
Read the sixteenth and seventeenth chapter of St Luke,
And you'll see how the lepers nine got their rebuke.
Ingratitude none of us do love,
And we may understand it is not desired above.
We have had many a good potato and corn crop before,
And for that few did God's kindness adore.

Janet Reid, 1846.

CARNOCK FAIR was held every year in Carnock on 26 May around the 'Thorn Cross' north of the Carnock Burn; and a cattle fair was held at the same time on the south side of the Burn. Lizz Mogg of Carnock describes Carnock Fair in *Carnock* (1989) a booklet printed privately for the pupils of Carnock Primary School:

> Every house, inside and outside was trim, redd [tidied] up and newly-washed for the Fair. Everyone from the surrounding countryside assembled to take part in the sports that animated the Haugh [a pasture] and the Square. It is said to have been a very lively occasion, with the music of pipers and fiddlers, dancing, feasting, and much merriment. Packmen would sell their wares and showmen would perform their plays and tricks. Races would be run and prizes of farls [thin oatmeal cakes] and gingerbread would be given.
>
> *Lizz Mogg*

The poem *On the Bonny Alley Tree* is found in Janet's chapbook entitled *Poems on Various Subjects* (1846). The words of *On the Bonny Alley Tree* indicate that Janet first visited Bridge of Allan five years earlier in 1841; and this poem also implies that she last visited Carnock in 1841. This interpretation accords with the record at the time of the national census on 6-7 June 1841 of Janet Reid staying in Torryburn which is 2 miles south of Carnock.

When Janet says: 'Come, pretty youths, come and see, Your picture in the Alley Tree', she is possibly referring to an artist who drew sketches for sale of the people attending Carnock Fair and who 'pitched' (pinned) the drawings to the Alley tree. 'My poor auld Jean' is also mentioned in Janet's poems *On Cruel Murder* and *On a Pleasant Young Gentleman* – Janet and 'poor auld Jean' may have lived together in Carnock until Jean died and perhaps this was another reason why Janet set off on her travels in 1840.

Janet composed several new poems that would appeal to the people of Carnock or Dunfermline when she decided to attend Carnock Fair in May 1846. She probably had these poems printed as broadsides by the Stirling Observer Office in readiness before she left Bridge of Allan. Carnock Fair came to an end in 1867 as trade gradually moved away to Dunfermline.

ON THE BONNY ALLEY TREE

The bonny Alley Tree was both straight and strong,
And it was the very one that was pitched upon.
Come, pretty youths, come and see,
Your picture in the Alley Tree.
There was many a tree that day stood in the den,
Resembled me and my poor auld* Jean. [old]
But the wind o'er them did lightly blaw*; [blow]
For it wasna' come to their time to fa'*. [fall]
The Alley Tree was the bonniest in all the raw*, [row]
But it was the first that got the fa'.
The bonny Alley Tree it soon fell down,
Just at the end of Carnock town.
This bonny tree minded me of a pretty youth –
In the year Eighteen Hundred and Thirty-Eight there rose a wind out o' the south,
And down fell the bonny tree that so resembled Youth.
Death often overtakes the young,
Although in youth they are fond o' fun.
We must all at last go like the Alley Tree –
You know it must be the case with both you and me.
Here we cannot always stay;
Like others we must go the way.
I would like young people always to remember,
That many a one never sees the month of December.
Many a genteel person calls upon me,
And I may thank God that I the Wells of Airthrey ere did see.
Poor people should always be content,
And thank God for every blessing that is sent.
Many a one more deserving than me,
Does not get a comfortable cup of tea.
For five long years have I been dwallin'
At the bonny Brig o' Allan.
Now I am returning back in wealth,
And, thank God for't, in good health.

Janet Reid, 1846.

ON THE REV. MR BRAND'S DEATH, IN DUNFERMLINE

Mr Brand died in the year Eighteen Hundred and Thirty-Eight,
And many a one for him had their cheeks to dight*; [wipe]
And I had mine to dight among the rest,
For aboon* all ministers I loved him best. [above]
To Fossoway Church I often did follow him,
And to Torryburn on the Mondays after him I did run.
But my running after him soon came to an end –
To spare him longer in this world God did not intend.
Death is the messenger of peace,
To call believers out of this world into a better place.
If anyone wishes his last text to see,
Read the second verse of the third chapter of Malachi.
Many a one the fifteenth Paraphrase will never forget,
While they in St Andrew's Church in Dunfermline sit.
The last words that in the pulpit he did sing
Was that 'Everlasting silence does reign'.
For his family and hearers, I do pity their case,
But I hope, through Christ's merits, they will meet him in a happy place.
As he for us and our minister did often pray,
I hope he will have many for a crown of rejoicing in that great day.
He took great care of his congregation that were young,
And I hope some good by them on his account will be done.
He likewise took great care of the distressed and poor,
And many a one laments him now I am sure.
There is but a meeting here, and to part again –
It is but a few short years any of us will on earth remain.
To one another we should always be discreet*, [obliging]
That in another and better world we may meet.
Man at first was made of dust,
And unto that man and woman return they must.

Janet Reid, 1846.

ON A PLEASANT YOUNG GENTLEMAN

This respectable Gentleman belongs to the West Neuk* of Fife,
Where I did spend the most part of my life. [Corner]
This Gentleman is Laird* of both houses and land, [Owner]
And of a great iron work, as I do understand.
He appears to be a Gentleman of very good respect –
And to take to himself a young lady I hope he'll not neglect –
I wish him a young lady clever and neat;
For a handsome young lady he'll have a good seat.
I wish him a lady of good nature,
For I see it in the gentleman's face in every feature.
As this Gentleman has plenty of money,
He will make some bonny young lady his honey –
And he to her will be just and true,
And that is what he never will rue.
And his lady to him will likely be the same,
And long together I wish they may remain.
It's a great sign of a Christian mind,
When husband and wife to each other are kind.
They will have servants at their demand,
And in kindness they will them command.
This Gentleman will likely marry a lady himself for to please,
And him and his lady will often ride in their chaise. [carriage]
Godliness is the promise of this life and that which is to come,
And to the poor, him and his lady will often spare a crumb.
The lady that was in the Blair of Carnock before,
Her for her kindness I did greatly adore –
She was very kind to me and my poor auld Jean,
And I hope kindness about the Blair will still be seen.
This gentleman is kind to my beloved minister, as I do understand,
It's surely a great blessing that e'er he stopt in Carnock land.
I hope this Gentleman will daily grow in grace –
The working people may be thankful that e'er he came to this place.
Now pleasant young Gentleman, I bid you adieu,
And I wish the blessing of God may aye remain with you.

Janet Reid, 1846.

ON 17 June 1847 *The Stirling Observer* refers to Janet Reid, though not by name, in an article by Paul Pry, Junior (the pseudonym of George E. McCulloch, a reporter of that newspaper):

> The Bridge of Allan! – a delightful watering place, as everyone knows […] now overflowing with the 'beauty and fashion' of the eastern and western metropolis who, having escaped from the smoke and dust, and hurry and bustle, and turmoil of 'the city' are there enjoying the beauties of this exquisite spot, where:
>
> The banks look gay in wild flowers clad,
> Beside the cooling hazel shade.
>
> and imbibing health and strength at the far-famed 'Airthrey Spring'. […] With its unrivalled walks, its lovely streams and wimpling burns, its 'Daurin' Road' [the Darn Walk beside the Allan Water between Bridge of Allan and Dunblane], and Airthrey braes, its commodious hotels, and its pleasant baths in its elegant villas, and its gallery of statuary, its well-furnished reading-room, and its incomparable poetess from Carnock. […] The Scottish Central Railway, now forming, will soon be completed, and then 'a' things will be right'. Only think, Sir, of the facility with which parties then may reach this watering-place, bringing, as it will bring, the cities of Edinburgh and Glasgow within little more than an hour's travel of the 'Bonny Brig o' Allan' […] to ruralise in the 'Wood of Kier', and adjacent sylvan scenes […]. Those who may yet travel by the Scottish Central have a rich treat awaiting them in their descent from the north, for, after leaving behind them the moss hags and peat bogs of Blackford and Strathallan, they enter a beautiful glen above the 'Mill o' Ash', and the run thence to Lecropt School is beautiful indeed. Skirting 'Allan Water' the whole way, and crossing it several times, the line is embosomed in hazel glades and hawthorn dales. […] Strange to say few of the inhabitants of Stirling avail themselves of the privilege within their reach.

Paul Pry, Junior, is probably quoting titles of more of Janet Reid's still undiscovered poems, probably those he bought from her: *Airthrey Spring*, *Daurin' Road*, *Bonny Brig o' Allan*, *Wood of Kier*, *Mill o' Ash* and *Allan Water* from which he quotes two lines!

ON GLASGOW'S BONNY CITY
(a new poem with a reused title)

I've travelled in Glasgow through many a street,
And the people in Glasgow to me were always discreet*. [obliging]
King William he at the Cross* does stand, [The Cross, Glasgow]
But no one now can he command.
Weapons of war by every man must be laid down,
But there is many a pretty soldier travels through Glasgow town.
In Glasgow I hope there is many a good Christian too,
I hope some good in their day all will do.
Glasgow people will not by any means be idle,
But I hope they will be often employed at their Bible.
Many good advices in the Bible are to be found,
And many chapters in it they will go round.
I hope they will read Christ's Sermon on the Mount,
And in every one of their actions at it point.
The first chapter of Isaiah there they will also see,
And kind unto the widow and fatherless they will always be.
They that unto the poor do give, unto the Lord do lend.
And God in His own time and way back will it send.
There are none who ever were losers by giving to the poor,
But many a one has been a loser by drinking I'm sure.
There's many a genteel person in Glasgow does dwell,
And many of them come along to Airthrey Well.
But the Drunken people to Airthrey Well they cannot win,
For their clothing on them turns most uncommon thin.
But many of the Glasgow people to righteousness do turn,
And for want they do not need for to mourn.
Godliness is the promise of this life and that which is to come,
And in Glasgow of righteous people there is always some.
For Glasgow's Bonny City I have a great respect,
And to make a poem on them I did not neglect.
Good people read your Testaments Old and New,
And that will teach everyone how to do.

Janet Reid, 1846.

MATTHEW BARR advertised the original opening of the 'Airthrey Wells Inn' in *The Scotsman* newspaper on 11 May 1839. The 'Grand Dinner' at the reopening of the Airthrey Wells Hotel described by Janet Reid in her poem *On Barr's Bonny Hotel* is reported in *The Caledonian Mercury* on Monday 20 July 1846:

> With the view of testifying to Mr Barr how much his endeavours to afford satisfaction have been appreciated, a number of gentlemen connected with the county, together with others who only occasionally visit the village, determined to celebrate the opening of the new place by giving him what is usually called a 'house warming' which was fixed to take place on Wednesday last. By the special permission of St Swithin (whose day it was) the weather was uncommonly fine which contributed in no small degree to heighten the enjoyment and to render it a complete holiday in the little place. Shortly before the hour for dinner, a stage coach arrived entirely fitted outside and in with a splendid military band playing the appropriate air of 'Come a' thegither' and immediately after alighting they took up their position on the balcony above the main entrance door which, together with the portico, was very tastefully decorated with flowers and evergreens, the whole surmounted by a large flag gracefully waving in the passing breeze. Dinner being announced by the sound of the gong, the company amounting to upwards of seventy repaired to the large room where every luxury of the season was abundantly and elegantly served up. […] Several gentlemen present sung a number of songs which […] contributed greatly to the pleasures of the evening. […] The company did not separate till a pretty late hour but it was the opinion of all to whom we spoke on the following day that there never was a more pleasant party than was at the opening dinner of the Airthrey Wells Hotel.

The 1851 national census of Bridge of Allan in the parish of Logie records Matthew Barr aged 36 'keeper' of the Hotel, his wife Isabella McQueen aged 37 and their children Matthew aged 9, John aged 7, Elizabeth aged 5 and Catherine aged 1 (James, Catherine's twin, had died). This accords with the family in Janet Reid's poem. The Airthrey Wells Hotel was renamed the Queen's Hotel in 1853 and it is still open but is now named the Adamo Hotel.

ON BARR'S BONNY HOTEL

This Hotel goes now under the name of Airthrey Well,
And long in it I wish him and his lady in prosperity to dwell.
They have two pretty little sons and a daughter too,
And I hope some good in their day they all will do.
They keep man and maid-servants of good respect,
And to wait on gentleman and lady they never do neglect.
Barr's name is on the door-head with blue and yellow,
And many a one says he is a trusty fellow.
And his wife is likewise of good respect,
And one another's welfare they never do neglect.
It is a very great sign of a Christian mind,
When husband and wife to each other are kind.
It is a very great sign of a growth in grace,
When people minds their Bible and live in peace.
There was always peace in their old Hotel before,
And on Sabbath days they have always kept a shut door.
And it is not far away from the Bowling-Green.
And I hope many a respectable gentleman and lady there will be seen.
There is a beautiful balcony on the door head,
And it will likely be seen after we are all dead.
A beautiful band of music on the balcony did play,
And there was a grand dinner at the opening of the Hotel that day.
Major Henderson in the chair that day did sit,
And for his fine speech many a cheer from the company he did get.
I hope Barr and his lady will always be kind to the poor,
And that is a good thing the Bible tells us we're sure.
Them that to the poor do give, unto the Lord does lend,
And He in His own time and way back will it send.
God can make anything prosper that comes in a Christian way,
And Barr and his lady have been very prosperous in their day.
This bonny Hotel was built in the year 'Forty-Six,
And I hope on the things in this world their minds they will not fix.
I hope in God's strength they will always prosper and thrive,
And do good to many one while they are alive.

Janet Reid, 1846.

ROBERT PHILP built his first Private Hotel (the villa now named 'Sunnyside') in 1835 opposite the future site of Barr's Hotel on Keir Street (the future Henderson Street) in Bridge of Allan.

The 1841 national census of Bridge of Allan in the parish of Lecropt records Robert Philp aged 35 'vintner', his wife Janet Nicol aged 30, their children James aged 4 and Robert aged 2 months, and Robert Philp's parents James Philp aged 75 and Isabella Philp aged 65, living in the Bridge of Allan Inn (now named the Old Bridge Inn) which was built in 1710 on the south side of the Stirling to Perth Road just west of the Old Brig over the Allan Water. The Inverallan Inn was also built in 1710 on the north side of the Stirling to Perth Road facing the Bridge of Allan Inn but it has been demolished.

So the 'mother' mentioned by Janet Reid in 1846 in her poem *On Philp's Bonny Royal Hotel* is Isabella Philp. The Old Parish Register records that the four Philp children in 1846 were James (born in 1837), William Honyseed (born in 1842), Robert (born in 1845 – the first Robert had died) and Isabella (born in 1846). William Honyseed's baptism on 20 January 1843 at Lecropt Church, Bridge of Allan, was witnessed by a 'Miss Reid' but this was almost certainly another lady and not Janet Reid the 'poetess' who was probably staying in Glasgow at this time.

The *Stirling Observer* for 23 June 1842 reports that: 'As the widening [extending] of the old bridge and levelling [raising] of the road are likely to impede the approach to Mr Philp's Bridge of Allan Inn, he has feued [leased] a space for a large inn and the office-houses at the east end of the village'. This became Philp's new Royal Hotel and its builders had a grand view of the Queen's carriage as it passed through Bridge of Allan on 13 September 1842. Sir Thomas Dick Lauder writes in his *Memorial of the Royal Progress in Scotland* (1843) that seventy-two horses were provided to pull (in relays) the Queen's carriage on the 20 mile journey from Drummond Castle near Crieff to Stirling Castle. Sir George Abercromby had two arches of tree trunks erected at the gate of Airthrey Castle and the group of guns within Sir George's grounds did not cease firing salutes as the Queen passed by until she reached Stirling Castle. The opening dinner of Philp's Royal Hotel was held on 2 June 1843. The Royal Hotel is still open in Bridge of Allan.

ON PHILP'S BONNY ROYAL HOTEL

It has two pretty pillars on each side of the door,
And beautiful bow windows, few like them I ever saw before.
This house is three stories high,
And many a one admires it as they pass by.
It is at the beginning o' the bonny Brig o' Allan,
Where many genteel people at present are dwallin'*. [dwelling]
The Hotel-keeper there has children four,
I hope in God's strength, prosperity they will have every day and
hour.
I hope Philp and his lady will daily grow in grace,
And be an honour, them and their family, in their own native place.
With their own industry they have built a bonny house,
And Philp and his lady are always sober and douce*. [respectable]
They have built a bonny addition to their Hotel, indeed,
And in prosperity I think they are coming speed.
There's a beautiful green before the addition's door,
And this bonny house stands a good way off from the sea shore.
Between Philp and his servants you will never hear any din;
And many a man and maid-servant are glad there to win.
Philp and his lady are kind to their mother dear,
And many a lady and gentleman after them will speer*. [enquire]
Through all the country they get a good name,
And for saying so people are not to blame.
They keep man and maid-servants of good respect –
To wait on gentlemen and ladies they never do neglect;
And many a one comes there on their marriage jaunt,
And good parlours and bedrooms they never will want.
A king to this bonny Hotel might bring his queen,
For there is about this bonny Hotel nothing that is mean.
For everything in it is fresh and new,
And I hope Philp and his family some good in it will do.
And although a marriage in it should soon take place,
Philp and his family will never count it a disgrace.

Janet Reid, 1846.

POEMS

ON

VARIOUS SUBJECTS.

BY JANET REID,

BRIDGE OF ALLAN.

PRINTED IN THE STIRLING OBSERVER OFFICE.

1846.

Glasgow University Library. *Janet Reid's chapbook* (*actual size*) *printed in the Stirling Observer Office, 1846.*

POEMS ON VARIOUS SUBJECTS Contents:

JOCK MACLEAN had this tribute paid to him (mentioning Janet Reid) in *The Stirling Observer* on Thursday 8 February 1855:

> 'Puir auld Jock Maclean' – as the well-known old man was wont to describe himself – has been gathered to his fathers, if he had any. He died some eight or ten days ago, in the pauper-hospital [work house]. Jock was a character, and though willing enough to let his wants be known, his importunity never got the length of making him disagreeable. […] Some eighty years ago, Jock was a herd-laddie on the Gowlin' Hills. Subsequently he took to the sea, and, having evidently a strong dash of the adventurous in his disposition, served for twelve or fourteen years on board a man-of-war. Whether he got his discharge, or took it, he was never willing to say […]. Jock was a great patron of the turf, and discovered […] at a somewhat late period of his life, that he had a genius for poetry, became the laureate of Stirling-races. […] Jock was one of the unlearned poets – his verses, indeed, were such as neither he himself nor any other person could read, but, he remarked quite philosophically: 'Things'll sing when they winna [won't] read'. There was only one word in the English language which he knew, and it he only knew on a sign: 'WHISKY'. Jock, indeed, had ceased at an early age to be a teetotaller, and soon ceased to be a moderate drinker too. He had been known to make six and seven shillings in a day by singing for pence at the starting place of the coaches, omnibuses and boats [in Stirling]; but, as the Yankee says, Jock *liquidated* his cash. The formation of the Scottish Central Railway he regarded with no favour, threatening, as it did, the 'vested interest' he possessed in the coaches. One of his most delightful ditties began:
>
> We'll a' be ruined noo,
> We'll a' be ruined noo,
> The railroad it has commenced,
> It's comin' through an' through!
>
> For a length of time Jock was public crier at Bridge of Allan, and next to the Lord of the Manor [facetiously meaning Major John Alexander Henderson] and Janet Reid, the only public character about the place. […] But Jock is gone, and, unless he had written his own epitaph, we know of no man equal to the task.

ON A JACK-DAW, ON THE BANKS OF THE ALLAN

This Jack-daw is a great pleasure for ladies and gentlemen to see,
And when they go about, it is a sight that is free.
In that village many a respectable person is dwelling,
When they go about the Water of Allan.
They keep lodgings neat and clean,
And no unrespectable thing about any of their houses is to be seen.
Strangers come from all the country round about,
And good lodgings the strangers soon find out.
They have churches new, where on Sundays they can meet,
And strangers to one another are always discreet.
And the inhabitants to the strangers are very kind too,
And they keep many a pleasant thing in the stranger's view.
And when at any time they wish a jaunt,
Servants and horses they will never want.
They will see the Rumbling Brig and the Cauthrin Linn,
Whenever they wish there to win.
Likewise they have many a pleasant walk through the woods so green,
And many pleasant walks about the Bridge of Allan is to be seen.
The strangers and the inhabitants always live in peace,
And I hope they will always grow in grace.
Many a one here recovers their health,
And many a one comes to the Bridge of Allan that has great wealth.
They have likewise hotels two,
And I hope them and the strangers good will do.
Now I bid you all farewell,
And I wish you help and happiness wherever you do dwell.
There is likewise another Jack-daw beside the fine hotel,
And many a respectable lady and gentleman comes there for a time to dwell.
Major Henderson and Mr Stirling of Keir,
Keep the working people always in good cheer.
When working people work can find,
They cannot be very far behind.

Janet Reid, 1850.

ON 8 December 1860 (six years after the death of Janet Reid) *The Caledonian Mercury*, an Edinburgh newspaper, printed a review by 'Jerrold' about *Innes's Domestic Poetry* (1857) comparing the sincere motives of Archibald Innes (who was a household servant) for composing poems to those of Janet Reid. Jerrold refers to her poems *Address to the Royal Family* and probably *On Domestic Happiness* both composed about 1850 but not found:

> We have read many volumes that have on their title pages claimed to be poems or poetry. We have met the late Mrs Janet Reid 'on the Banks of Allan Water' and in the pages of her works. Janet had an abiding belief in her poetic powers; and as most poets have certain pet brain-children […] even so Janet dilated with parental fondness on her 'Address to The Royal Family'. It was only to the favoured few she *in propria persona* – and she was a very proper person – chanted of how:
>
> > The Queen and Prince Albert passed through the Bridge of Allan,
> > Where at present a number of respectable persons are dwalling.
>
> And her lines on 'Domestic Happiness':
>
> > Around the tea-table there is contentment and peace
> > When you get a pious individual to say the grace;
> > For the human mind nothing possibly better enjoys
> > Than a comfortable fireside where there isn't any noise.
>
> Mrs Reid was a decent douce wife, but she was not a poet. To the individual who has never possessed the sense of smell, the perfume of a bean field in July and the effluvia of a corrupting marsh in the same month are undistinguishable. In the judgement of the aforesaid lady there was no gradation, no ascent or descent from Shakespeare to Janet Reid; it was one level, lofty or low. Her art of poetry was resolved into, as she termed it: 'a guid clink' [a good rhyme or, more likely, a good money-earner]. She wrote neither for antiquity nor posterity, but for the penny. If her productions were bought she heeded not if the purchaser never perused them. She was the worst would-be poet we ever met. She is dead – peace to her ashes. […] She was a pot-boiler poet, and dashed into print whenever her larder was low.
>
> *Jerrold*

ON THE YEAR 1853

This is now another New Year,
And many of us on earth do yet appear.
We should all learn contented for to be,
For many an alteration every year we see.
In our short day we should never be idle,
But very often employed at our Bible.
The Scriptures we should all understand,
For we may soon get our call by sea or by land.
We should set our hearts beyond the grave,
As we know not on earth how few days we may have.
Remember what our Saviour to Mary did say,
The part she had chosen would ne'er be taken away.
Often think on Christ's sufferings in the Garden and on the Tree*,
How he suffered for sinners such as you and me. [Cross]
Read Christ's Sermon on the Mount,
And in every one of your actions at it point.
Read the thirty-seventh Psalm,
And to one another be always kind and calm,
Them that have families read and pray,
And lead young ones on the heavenly way.
Read your Testaments Old and New,
And that will teach us all what to do.
This is the year 'Fifty-Three,
And it may finish the earthly course with either you or me
Man at first was made of dust,
And man and woman return to it they must.

Janet Reid, 1853.

[See overleaf Robert Louis Stevenson's first visit to Bridge of Allan in 1853 and his possible encounter with Janet Reid]

ROBERT LEWIS BALFOUR STEVENSON (1850-1894) came as a 3-year old to Bridge of Allan with his parents in May 1853 for the first of many times in his youth. He was known to them as 'Lewis' or 'Smout' (which is Scots for the young of a salmon). His parents later changed the spelling (though not the pronunciation) of his name to 'Louis' and he dropped the name 'Balfour' as an adult. Robert Louis Stevenson writes in *Memoirs of Himself* written in 1880 though published posthumously on his instructions:

> But the time when my mind displayed most activity was after I was put to bed and before I fell asleep. I remember these periods more distinctly and I believe further back than any other part of my childhood. I would lie awake declaiming aloud to myself my views on the universe in something I called singing although I have no ear and in a measure of my own although at that time I can have known nothing of verse. One of these 'songstries', for I named my evening exercises, was taken down by my father from behind the door […] But what is truly odd, it fell into a loose, irregular measure with a tendency toward the ten-syllable heroic line. This, as I am sure I can then have heard little or nothing but hymn metres, seems to show a leaning in the very constitution of the language to that form of verse; or was it but a trick of the ear, inherited from eighteenth century ancestors?
>
> *Robert Louis Stevenson*

Margaret Isabella Balfour Stevenson (1829-1897) Smout's mother, in her notes for 1 September 1855 written by hand in her book entitled *Baby's Record*, probably quotes from one of Smout's 'songstries' under the heading 'Smout's Poetry':

No sun is in the sky
While night comes on
Then stars and moon comes out
And then another day
The sun comes out again.

Graham Balfour, Robert Louis Stevenson's cousin, in *The Life of Robert Louis Stevenson* (1901) reproduces the 'songstrie' in 'a loose, irregular measure with a tendency toward the ten-syllable heroic line', that was taken down by Smout's father, Thomas Stevenson (1818-1877) and dated 23 April 1857:

Had not an angel got the pride of man,
No evil thought, no hardened heart would have been seen.
No hell to go;
That angel was the Devil.
Had not the angel got the pride, there would have been no need
For Jesus Christ to die upon the Cross.

John Howell, San Francisco, published *Stevenson's Baby Book being the Record of the Sayings and Doings of Robert Louis Balfour Stevenson, son of Thomas Stevenson and Margaret Isabella Balfour or Stevenson* in 1922 as an edition of 500 facsimile copies of the *Baby's Record* by 'R.I.W.' printed and published by Field & Tuer, The Leadenhall Press, with sub-headings which Margaret Isabella Stevenson had filled in by hand. She also added notes, starting with 1851 at the end of which she writes: '*Diary for '52 lost*' and continues with her notes for 1853 to 1858. Later she writes that she has found the lost diary and she inserts the notes for 1852.

Stevenson's Baby Book ... has a preface written by Katherine D. Osbourne the first wife (who he later divorced) of Lloyd Osbourne, Robert Louis Stevenson's stepson:

> This Baby Record was meant by the young mother who wrote it, as all such Records are, to keep, for memory's sake, an account of the first few years of her adored child. A few of the notes were added by her in later years. [...] With every passing year his Baby Record grew a more precious possession to the mother.

This statement is not true though Katharine may not have realised that for she was given the *Baby's Record* by Jane Whyte Balfour, Margaret Isabella Balfour Stevenson's sister, after Margaret had died. There are anomalies in the notes put in this record for the book was not actually compiled until much later.

Matthew McLennan Young in *Field & Tuer, The Leadenhall Press: A Checklist* (2010) writes that this firm of printers published its own books between 1862 and 1905 and that 'Ltd' was added to their name from 1892. The *Baby's Record* by 'R.I.W.' (no Ltd) was first published in July 1889 and the author is given as the Rev. Reginald Illingworth Woodhouse in the revised (second) edition published in 1895. Stevenson's *Baby's Record* is a first edition of 1889 and it must have been bought by his mother in Edinburgh soon after she returned from Vailima on Upolo in Samoa after her son's death in December 1894. So Margaret Isabella Stevenson, as an aged and grieving mother, compiled this *Baby's Record* of her only child (later the author Robert Louis Stevenson) in retrospect in 1895.

Alison Cunningham (1822-1913) or 'Cummy' became Smout's much-loved nurse when he was 18 months old. Alison was born in Torryburn 2 miles south of Carnock. She was devout and would have gone to the tiny kirk in Torryburn that Janet Reid describes going to in her poem *On the Rev. Mr Brand's Death, in Dunfermline*. Janet would also have sold her broadsides in Torryburn.

Margaret Isabella Stevenson wrote a note in her *Baby's Record* about their first visit to Bridge of Allan: '*May 20th* [*1853*]: *Smout at Free Church, Bridge of Allan, with Cummy and was very good*'. Janet Reid would probably have gone to this church service too.

Perhaps 'Cummy' and 'Smout' walked to the Airthrey Well House in May and June 1853. Alison Cunningham would have recognised Janet Reid from her visits to Torryburn. Perhaps they greeted each other despite the difference in their ages. Perhaps Cummy and Smout listened to Janet 'chaunting' her 'unpolished' poems – which are composed in 'a loose, irregular measure with a tendency toward the ten-syllable heroic line'. So was it Janet's 'chaunting' of her poems that so impressed itself on young Smout's mind?

'Smout' in 1854 from 'Stevenson's Baby Book'.

ON AIRTHREY WELL HOUSE.

The people here keep baths of different kinds three,
Which will answer people of high or low degree;
Likewise good lodgings for visitors they do prepare,
The strangers in good usage they will always share;
And they can take a walk around the house,
And the people that belong to it are always sober and douse.
The strangers can walk about at their leasure,
And pull a bonny flower at their pleasure;
There they can pull the brier that grows so sweet,
And the people there, and strangers, are always discreet;
And in the corner there grows a bonny bunch of honeysuckle,
Perhaps young people there in marriage may buckle.
Its long since marriage was the fashion in our Scotch land,
And likewise in England as we do understand.
When people comes about this country,
Perhaps a choice for themselves they may see;
And if it be their fortune for to be wed,
To see them comfortable I will be very glad.
I must now turn to the house that near the Well does stand,
And the master and mistress has servants at their command,
Likewise a pretty little daughter that they lead in their hand—
This child is but young yet, as we do understand.
I hope this little child will grow in grace,
And be an honour to all her friends about the place.
This child may yet be a lady,
And I hope she will get a husband when once she is ready.
I hope her parents will set before her a good example,
And if she lives till she is old she will likely keep the sample.
Her parents are both of very good respect,
And the poor and needy's case they never do neglect.
The strangers will see this bonny house as they pass by,
And it is a bonny house no strangers will deny.
The six corners of the house I cannot get in,
And to spoil my poem I need not begin.

JANET REID, Carnock, Fifeshire.

Printed in the Stirling Observer Office.

Peter Forbes' album. *Printed in the Stirling Observer Office, 1843.*
[*See the poem on page 71*]

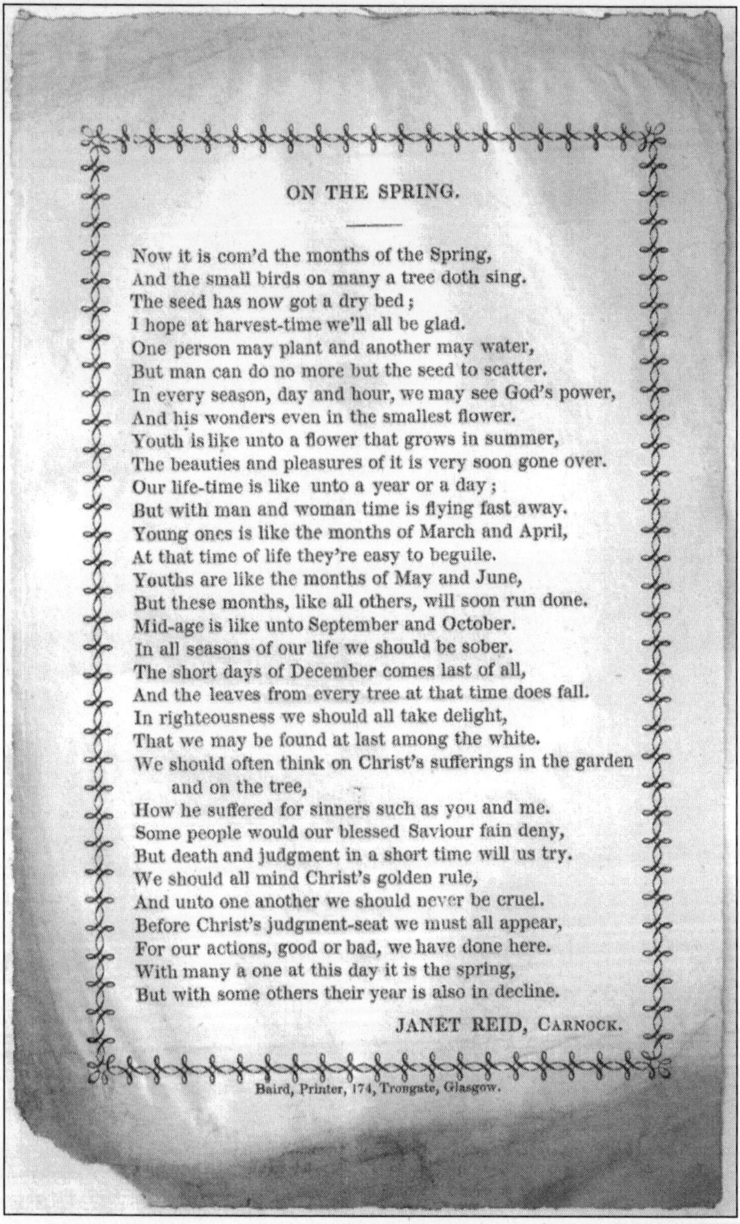

ON THE SPRING.

Now it is com'd the months of the Spring,
And the small birds on many a tree doth sing.
The seed has now got a dry bed;
I hope at harvest-time we'll all be glad.
One person may plant and another may water,
But man can do no more but the seed to scatter.
In every season, day and hour, we may see God's power,
And his wonders even in the smallest flower.
Youth is like unto a flower that grows in summer,
The beauties and pleasures of it is very soon gone over.
Our life-time is like unto a year or a day;
But with man and woman time is flying fast away.
Young ones is like the months of March and April,
At that time of life they're easy to beguile.
Youths are like the months of May and June,
But these months, like all others, will soon run done.
Mid-age is like unto September and October.
In all seasons of our life we should be sober.
The short days of December comes last of all,
And the leaves from every tree at that time does fall.
In righteousness we should all take delight,
That we may be found at last among the white.
We should often think on Christ's sufferings in the garden
and on the tree,
How he suffered for sinners such as you and me.
Some people would our blessed Saviour fain deny,
But death and judgment in a short time will us try.
We should all mind Christ's golden rule,
And unto one another we should never be cruel.
Before Christ's judgment-seat we must all appear,
For our actions, good or bad, we have done here.
With many a one at this day it is the spring,
But with some others their year is also in decline.

JANET REID, CARNOCK.

Baird, Printer, 174, Trongate, Glasgow.

Peter Forbes' album. *Printed by Hugh Baird, Glasgow, 1840.*

[*See the poem on page 39*]

NOTES

Page 37: ON THE HONOURABLE MANUFACTURERS OF DUNFERMLINE

On the Honourable Manufacturers of Dunfermline was composed by Janet Reid probably in 1837. The broadside has no printer's imprint and it was probably printed in 1840 but not in Dunfermline. The number of weavers in Scotland rose from 8,500 in 1792 to 84,000 by 1838 and the weaving of linen became a major industry. Initially the weavers' earnings were high but they declined with the use of mechanised looms. Ebenezer Henderson writes in *The Annals of Dunfermline and Vicinity from the earliest Authentic Period to the Present Time* (1879) that there were over 3,000 looms in Dunfermline by 1837. A severe trade depression peaked in the winter of 1837-38 resulting in over 600 unemployed weavers in Dunfermline. Andrew J. Campbell in *Fife Shopkeepers and Traders (1820-1870)* (1989) gives details of the manufacturers that are found in the directories and newspaper advertisements of Fife during that period. David Dewar or John Dewar, John Cooper, William Hunt, and George Walker, Fergusson ('Fergie' who left in 1837) and James Bryce were linen-manufacturers. In 1833 Erskine Beveridge (1803-1864) began weaving damask-linen. Peter Forbes gave the only broadside found of this poem to Erskine Beveridge, Junior (1853-1920) who in turn gave it to Dunfermline Carnegie Library.

Page 39: ON THE SPRING

On the Spring was composed by Janet Reid possibly in 1837.

Page 41: LAMENT FOR A BELOVED MINISTER

Lament for a Beloved Minister was composed by Janet Reid in 1837 about Thomas Gray Duncan who probably assisted the Rev. William Forfar in Saline (he was aged 81 in 1837) as a 'missionary'. Thomas Gray Duncan became the first minister of St David's Church in Kirkintilloch which opened on 8 June 1837. Kirkintilloch is 7 miles from Glasgow and 27 miles from Saline or Carnock.

Page 42: ON A COMFORTABLE CUP OF TEA

On a Comfortable Cup of Tea was composed by Janet Reid possibly in 1838. One of the five different broadsides can be read online under *The Word on the Street* on the website of the National Library of Scotland.

Page 43: ON CHILDREN GOING TO CHURCH

On Children Going to Church was composed by Janet Reid possibly as early as 1838 for the broadside is the 15th 'Edition' printed in 1843. Janet says in this poem that: 'This was done by one who never was at school'. She also recalls the annual Communion services that were held in the Haugh (a pasture beside the Carnock Burn) in Carnock from 1619 to 1823 when they were stopped because: 'There was much drunken behaviour'. A 'tent' (a wooden 'field-pulpit' standing on four legs with a pitched roof, like a sentry-box) was erected beside the 'Queen of the Haugh' (a large beech tree in the pasture) and the congregation sat on the 'Preachers' Braes' (the grassy slopes beside the Carnock burn). This 'tent' was found in an outhouse at the Carnock manse in the 1940s and it is now in the National Museum of Scotland, Edinburgh.

Page 45: ON HUMILITY

On Humility was composed by Janet Reid possibly as early as 1838. Two of the broadsides of this poem are duplicate copies of the 'Eleventh Edition' printed by Thomas Graham (the partner of John Neilson) in Paisley possibly in 1842 on Janet's second visit to Paisley. The typefaces used for the text and for the printer's imprint on Janet Reid's broadsides printed by either John Neilson or Thomas Graham in Paisley are identical.

Page 47: ON GIVING WORK TO WORKING FOLK

On Giving Work to Working Folk was composed by Janet Reid in Carnock possibly in 1839. The broadside of this poem was printed by Hugh Baird in Glasgow probably in 1840 with Janet's home put as 'Carnock'. The 'worthy Gentleman' in this poem may have been John A. Stuart who was the laird (owner) from 1838 to 1854 of Carnock House (built circa 1550, improved in 1827 and demolished in 1941). Janet says in this poem: 'Because the pen, that valuable thing, I never could use'. Carnock, like Saline, was a centre of weaving in the early 1800s and the Rev William Gilston reports in the *New Statistical Account of Scotland* (compiled 1834-45) that in 1841 in the parish of Carnock (including the villages of Carnock and Cairneyhill) there were 205 persons employed in weaving comprising 155 males and 50 females; and that there were 208 looms in the parish of Carnock and 159 of these were Jacquard machines and the others were hand-looms.

Page 49: ON CRUEL MURDER

On Cruel Murder was composed by Janet Reid in Carnock possibly in 1839. The first Ordnance Survey map (1856) shows a corn mill in Carnock with a mill-pond on the Carnock Burn. Torryburn is on the Firth of Forth 2 miles south of Carnock. 'Bennie' (a Scottish surname) is not in the 1841 census of Carnock. The 'old woman' may be 'poor auld Jean' who is named in Janet's poems. The broadside of this poem is attached by mistake to a medical pamphlet in the Wellcome Library for the History & Understanding of Medicine, London. Over 100 broadsides about hangings (one in ten of them of women) before thousands of spectators from the early 1800s to 1868 (when they ceased in public) are viewable on *The Word on the Street* on the website of the National Library of Scotland. A third are hangings on the Lawn Market in Edinburgh; another third are in Glasgow; and the other third are in Stirling, Ayr, Paisley or Aberdeen, or sometimes at the site of the crime.

Page 51: ON THE GALLANT SAILORS

On the Gallant Sailors was composed by Janet Reid possibly on a visit to Kirkcaldy, Fife, in 1839. The Rev. George Bell Brand (1786-1838) was the minister of St Andrew's Church in Dunfermline. The Rev. John Willison (1680-1750) went to London in 1734 seeking the repeal of patronage in the Church of Scotland. The Rev. Thomas Boston (1676-1732) was a Scottish theologian. The Rev. William Dyer was a nonconformist minister in Chesham, England, who died in 1696 but his sermons were reprinted in Glasgow in 1761. 'Wilson' as put by mistake in the penultimate line of the earliest broadside is changed to 'Willison' in an 1842 printing of the poem.

Page 52: ON THE GALLANT SHOEMAKERS

On the Gallant Shoemakers was composed by Janet Reid in 1839 possibly in Kirkcaldy judging from the title and from her farewell: 'I bid you all adieu' which Janet also used in *On the Gallant Sailors.*

Page 53: ON THE MID-MILL

On the Mid-Mill was composed by Janet Reid in 1840. In the 1841 national census, Laurie (Laurence) Wilson aged 53 a 'flax- spinner', his wife Janet aged 50 and their son Thomas aged 14 an 'agricultural labourer' are living in the Mid-Mill by the Lynne Burn on the road to Pitliver House 3 miles south of Dunfermline.

Page 56: ON GLASGOW, BONNY TOWN or ON GLASGOW'S BONNY CITY

On Glasgow, Bonny Town was composed by Janet Reid when she first visited Glasgow in 1840. The earliest broadside is entitled *On Glasgow, Bonny Town* printed by Hugh Baird in Glasgow. This same poem is entitled *On Glasgow's Bonny City* when it was printed by William Gilchrist as the 'Seventh Edition' dated 'Glasgow, April 1842'. The 'Eighth Edition' was one of 10 broadsides printed in the same batch by the Stirling Observer Office towards the end of 1842 before Janet left Bridge of Allan to visit Glasgow where her poem *For the New-Year* was composed at the beginning of 1843. These 10 broadsides are now kept in Dunfermline Carnegie Library. This batch shows that Janet Reid changed her home from 'Carnock' to 'Carnock, Fifeshire' in late 1842. Edwin Chadwick (1800-1890) shows in *An Inquiry into the Sanitary Conditions of the Labouring Population of Great Britain* (1842) the link between poor sanitation and disease. He writes that Glasgow was: 'Possibly the filthiest and unhealthiest of the British towns'. Infant mortality in Glasgow was the highest in Great Britain at that time with half of the children living there dying before the age of 5 years.

Page 57: ON PRETTY PAISLEY

On Pretty Paisley was composed by Janet Reid in 1840. The first 7 miles of the Glasgow, Paisley, Kilmarnock and Ayr Railway, operated jointly with the Glasgow, Paisley & Greenock Railway and known as the Glasgow & Paisley Joint Railway opened between Glasgow and Paisley on 27 July 1840. So Janet Reid almost certainly arrived in Paisley on 15 September 1840. Janet probably travelled by rail for the first time on this visit. The broadside of *On Pretty Paisley* was printed by Thomas Graham the partner of John Neilson probably on her second visit to Paisley in 1842.

Page 59: ON THE YEAR 1841

On the Year 1841 was composed by Janet Reid at the beginning of that year. The broadside is a recent acquisition by the National Library of Scotland, Edinburgh. Janet's home is put as 'Carnock' but it has no printer's imprint. Perhaps it was printed in Falkirk (a centre of the iron-casting industry at that time) which she could have visited and where she could have stayed on her journey from Glasgow to Bridge of Allan via Stirling.

Page 63: ON AIRTHREY WATER

On Airthrey Water was probably composed by Janet Reid in 1841. The broadside was printed in 1843 in the Stirling Observer Office by which time Janet was putting her home as 'Carnock, Fifeshire'. The 'Airthrey Water' flowed from three springs in an abandoned copper-mine beneath the Ochil Hills above Bridge of Allan. Sir Robert Abercromby (1740-1827) laird (owner) of the Airthrey Estate had the water analysed in 1820 by Dr Thomson, Professor of Chemistry at Glasgow University, who reported that: 'No mineral water of its class in Great Britain could approach the Bridge of Allan water in its medicinal qualities'. Airthrey mineral water was clear and it had no smell but it had an unpleasant and bitter taste and it was an effective purgative.

Page 65: ON DUNBLANE

On Dunblane was composed by Janet Reid in Dunblane in 1841 on her first visit which she would have made about the same time as she made her first visit to Bridge of Allan. The broadside was printed by William Gilchrist in Glasgow with the date '1842' put as a footnote. The roof of the nave of the Cathedral in Dunblane fell down after the Reformation in 1560 (probably following neglect) and it was not restored until 1893. Mineral-water springs were discovered in 1813 in Cromlix 2 miles from Dunblane but they were not developed until the 1870s.

Page 66: IN SPEAKING BE MILD

In Speaking Be Mild was composed by Janet Reid possibly in 1841. Janet alludes to the 'mote and beam' in the Bible. The broadside was printed by Thomas Graham (the partner of John Neilson) in Paisley probably on her second visit in 1842.

Page 67: ON THE YEAR FORTY-TWO

On the Year Forty-Two was composed by Janet Reid at the start of 1842 probably while she was visiting Glasgow. This poem is in Janet's chapbook entitled *Poems on Various Subjects* which she had printed in the Stirling Observer Office in 1846 (even though she had composed New Year poems for 1843 and 1844 and probably 1845). William Gilchrist in Glasgow printed the 24th edition of her poem *On a Comfortable Cup of Tea* with the footnote 'Glasgow, March 1842' so she was certainly in Glasgow by that date.

MELANCHOLY ACCIDENT.

The Telegraph, new high pressure engine steam boat,
When not far from Helensburgh Quay did float,
A melancholy accident has been,
The like about this place before was never seen.
This Steamer and the Railroad, I understand, were trying a race;
People for gain one another should never chase.
If people cannot gain a sixpence, they should be content with a groat,
For it is sometimes dangerous when folks on the water do float.
By what our Saviour at the Tower of Siloam did say,
We should speak cautiously, let the case be what it may.
As the tree falleth, so must it lie;
To lead a righteous life every body should try.
There are many in Glasgow and Greenock now will weep,
When they think that friends and acquaintances in death doth sleep.
I hope many of their friends hereafter will see,
Where sun nor moon will never need to be.
This happened in the year eighteen hundred and forty-two,
When folks about railways and steamers made so much ado.
When in the mornings people do rise,
Sometimes ere night they meet a sad surprise;
And many a one has gone well to bed at night,
And never again hath seen the morning light.
Oh, may we all remember, every day,
That time with every one is flying fast away.
The 14th and 15th Paraphrase I advise you to read,
And with sober people always to take up your head
The Scriptures we should all try to understand,
For we know not whether our call may be by sea or land.
It was on March 21st, the boiler of this steamer at Helensburgh did
burst,
When worthy Captain Ewing, with the gallant crew and passengers,
into the sea were thrust.
We should always set our hearts beyond the grave,
Where through Christ's sufferings pleasures we evermore may have.

JANET REID, Carnock.

Gilchrist, Printer, Glasgow.

Peter Forbes' album. *Printed by William Gilchrist, Glasgow, 1842.*

[*See the poem on page 68*]

Page 68: MELANCHOLY ACCIDENT

Melancholy Accident was composed by Janet Reid soon after 21 March 1842 and the broadside was printed by William Gilchrist in Glasgow. Janet probably misunderstood about the locomotive engine from the report in *The Glasgow Courier* headed: 'Explosion of the Telegraph Steamer at Helensburgh and Melancholy Loss of Life' which says that the *Telegraph* was a relatively fast wooden paddle-steamer with a high-pressure locomotive engine that was built on the River Clyde in 1841 by Hedderwick & Ransome: 'For the purpose of competing with the railway'. The *Telegraph* left the Broomielaw at 10 am on 21 March 1842 bound for Greenock and Helensburgh and Rosneath. The boiler exploded as the paddles began to turn again while the ship was still alongside the pier in Helensburgh 20 miles west of Glasgow. Among the 20 people killed were her Captain William Ewing and Mr Hedderwick the builder of the paddle-steamer (everyone else on board was injured). The wooden piers could hold only one steamer at a time and they did race each other. Captain James Williamson in *The Clyde Passenger Steamer* (1904) writes that: 'There is little room for doubt that some of the deplorable accidents which occurred about this time were attributable to this fierce rivalry. Among these [was] the explosion of the *Telegraph* at Helensburgh in 1842'.

Page 69: AGAINST SABBATH BREAKERS

Against Sabbath Breakers was composed in 1842 in Glasgow after the Edinburgh and Glasgow Railway opened on 21 February 1842. Construction of the 35-mile long Forth and Clyde Canal with 39 locks began in 1768 and it opened over its full length including a Branch to Port Dundas Basin, Glasgow, in 1790. The 32 mile long Union Canal opened in 1822 and this was constructed along the 240 foot contour from Edinburgh with an 11-lock flight at Falkirk (now replaced by the Falkirk Wheel) for the descent to the Forth and Clyde Canal. By 1836 these two canals were carrying 200,000 passengers a year between Edinburgh and Glasgow. The Edinburgh and Glasgow Railway opened in 1842 and it ran partly alongside the Forth and Clyde Canal. By 1848 all passenger traffic on the Union Canal and the Forth and Clyde Canal had ceased. In 1846 the North British Railway Company ended its Sunday rail services on the Edinburgh and Glasgow Railway following religious pressure.

Page 71: ON AIRTHREY WELL HOUSE

On Airthrey Well House was composed by Janet Reid in 1842 when the child, Janet, daughter of John Halley and Margaret McPherson born on 31 March 1841 was beginning to walk. John Halley was the keeper of the Well House in the 1841 census. Janet Halley died in infancy. The first part of this poem is about the Bath House and the second part is about the Well House. An advertisement by James Miller (lessee of the Bath House and the Well House) in the 3rd edition 1853 of the guide *A Week at Bridge of Allan* by Charles Roger gives the charges for the use of Airthrey Mineral Water (available only at the Well House): a hot plunge bath 2s (shillings) 0d (old pence); a cold bath 1s 6d; a tepid shower 1s 6d; or a cold shower 1s 0d. The charges for using fresh water (available at both the Well House and the Bath House) are: a hot plunge bath 1s 6d; a cold bath 1s 0d; a tepid shower 1s 0d; or a cold shower 0s 9d.

Page 73: ON THE BONNY BRIG O'ALLAN

On the Bonny Brig o' Allan was composed by Janet Reid in 1842 when an 'addition' (a third arch for a lade or mill-stream) was built to the Old Brig over the Allan Water. The *Stirling Observer* on 23 June 1842 reports the raising of the approaches to the Old Brig. Janet changed the words from: 'On the left side of the road they see what grew for sin' in her chapbook *Poems on Various Subjects* (1846) to: 'On the left side of the road you'll see a new town begin' in a broadside printed around 1850. Perhaps Janet was alluding to the sin of Sabbath-breaking by the builders of the new villas.

Page 75: FOR YOUNG LADIES

For Young Ladies was composed by Janet Reid probably in Bridge of Allan in mid-1842. Queen Victoria was crowned on 20 June 1837 at 18 years of age. The three Kings were: George III reigned 1760-1820; George IV (the eldest son of George III) reigned 1820-1830; and William IV (third son of George III) reigned 1830-1837.

Page 76: FOR GENTLEMEN OR LADIES or FOR LADIES OR GENTLEMEN

For Gentlemen or Ladies was composed by Janet Reid probably in Bridge of Allan in mid-1842. The title of this poem was either varied by Janet to attract the respective buyers or it was changed to *For Ladies or Gentlemen* sometime between 1843 and 1846.

Page 77: FOR BACHELORS

For Bachelors was composed by Janet Reid probably in Bridge of Allan in mid-1842 after Janet composed *For Young Ladies.*

Page 79: ON AN ACCIDENT AT THE BRIG O' ALLAN

On an Accident at the Brig o' Allan was composed by Janet Reid soon after 18 June 1842. Possibly the accident occurred at the Airthrey Paper Mills on the Allan Water where accidents did happen. Cornelius was a Roman Centurion in the Bible. Janet gave the profit from selling this broadside to the injured man's family.

Page 80: ON VANITY FAIR

On Vanity Fair was composed by Janet Reid in Bridge of Allan soon after 6 August 1842. The racecourse was built in 1805 in the King's Park, Stirling, but horse-racing there was stopped in 1854 as an 'undesirable pastime'. Perhaps Janet went to the races to sell her broadsides. By 1851 Major Henderson had become the 'Principal of the Fraternity of Chapmen' a guild of Stirling traders established in 1423 by James I, King of Scots. 'The Valley' on the south side of Stirling Castle Hill was used for open-air 'tent' preaching.

Page 81: ON DRAPERS AND GROCERS

On Drapers and Grocers was composed soon after 29 August 1842 when the Nanking Treaty was signed ending the First Opium War 1839-42 with China. Tea was brought from China by East Indiamen in the 1840s and by the faster Clipper ships in the 1850s-60s.

Page 83: A CHECK FOR SCOFFERS

A Check for Scoffers was composed by Janet Reid soon after 1 September 1842 when Queen Victoria and Prince Albert arrived in Leith, Edinburgh. Queen Victoria and Prince Albert had sailed from London to Granton Harbour (opened in 1838) Leith on the Royal Yacht HMS *Royal George* (a naval paddle-steamer) with two frigate escorts to avoid the risk of Chartist riots in the North of England. The Queen and Prince Albert then crossed the Firth of Forth by the Queensferry Passage. In *Queen Victoria's Highland Journals* (1968) the Queen writes: 'Captain Wemyss, elder brother of General Wemyss [the Queen's equerry], rode with us all the way beyond Cowdenbeath'. Captain James Erskine Wemyss RN., MP. was Lord Lieutenant of Fife, 1840-54. Janet Reid composed a poem for him, remember, in 1837!

Page 85: THE QUEEN'S FAREWELL

The Queen's Farewell was composed by Janet Reid soon after Queen Victoria and Prince Albert passed through Bridge of Allan on 13 September 1842 on the return journey from their first holiday in the Scottish Highlands. Sir Thomas Dick Lauder writes in his *Memorial of the Royal Progress in Scotland* (1843) that three triumphal arches were erected in Bridge of Allan: one at the inn (the Bridge of Allan Inn in Lecropt); one at the turnpike gate (at the east end of the Old Brig); and one at the Reading-Room which had a bee-hive and a bee and the motto: 'How doth our good Queen bee improve each shining hour', a parody of: 'How doth the little busy bee / Improve each shining hour' from the poem 'Against Idleness and Mischief ' in *Divine and Moral Songs for the Use of Children* (1715) composed by the Rev. Isaac Watts (1674-1748).

Page 87: FOR THE NEW-YEAR

For the New-Year was composed by Janet Reid at the beginning of 1843. The broadside was printed in 1843 by William Gilchrist of Glasgow with Janet's home put as 'Carnock, Fifeshire'.

Page 89: ON THE FAITHFUL MINISTERS OF THE CHURCH OF SCOTLAND

On the Faithful Ministers of the Church of Scotland was composed after January 1843 when Parliament rejected a claim by the Church of Scotland against patronage; and probably before the Disruption in the Church of Scotland on 18 May 1843. The Old Kirk in Carnock was founded in the twelfth century and it was rebuilt in 1602 when the roof of heather was replaced by slate. It was condemned in 1838 and its ruin still stands in the old burial ground where gravestones are engraved with 'mortality symbols' of a skull and cross-bones or with 'trade emblems': an anvil on a blacksmith's gravestone or a goose (pressing-iron) and shears on a tailor's gravestone. The Rev. Thomas Gillespie (1708-1774) was the minister of Carnock from 1741 to 1752. He was deposed by the General Assembly of the Church of Scotland because he refused to induct a new minister in Inverkeithing in 1749 who was opposed by the congregation. In Strathbogie seven ministers were deposed in 1841 for accepting the decision of a secular court. In Auchterarder the congregation rejected the patron's nominee in 1834 in a dispute that went on appeal to the House of Lords.

Page 90: ON RESPECTABLE BAKERS

On Respectable Bakers was composed by Janet Reid probably in early 1843 in Edinburgh. Janet most likely travelled there by the Glasgow to Edinburgh railway. The broadside of *On Respectable Bakers* has no printer's imprint but it was printed by the Macdonald family in Edinburgh for it uses the same typeface and has the same printers' flowers as a broadside of *On Edinburgh City* which has a Macdonald imprint. It was most likely the printer who made a pun of '*bred*' by putting the word in italic type for Janet uses the term 'well bred' to mean polite in *On Giving Work to Working Folk* and *On the Gallant Shoemakers*.

Page 91: ON EDINBURGH CITY

On Edinburgh City was composed by Janet Reid in Edinburgh probably on her second visit in early 1843. A broadside was printed by Macdonald in Edinburgh probably in 1843 with Janet's home put as 'Carnock, Fifeshire'. The Railway Company ended its rail services on the Sabbath in 1846 following religious pressure. In this poem Janet says that she: 'Never learned to use' a pen and that she dictated her poems. Edwin Chadwick writes in *An Inquiry into the Sanitary Conditions of the Labouring Population of Great Britain* (1842) that families moved to Edinburgh in the early 1800s after the clearances from the Highlands of Scotland. They lived in single rooms in tall and crowded stone tenements without a water supply. The streets of the Old Town in Edinburgh were open sewers and deaths from 'fever' (cholera) were prevalent. Edwin Chadwick campaigned for better-ventilated and less-crowded housing, a piped water supply and piped disposal of sewage.

Page 95: BE MERCIFUL TO BODY AND TO BEAST

Be Merciful to Body and to Beast was composed by Janet Reid probably in Bridge of Allan in mid-1843 when the broadside was printed. A 'wanded creel' was possibly a horse-drawn carriage built of cane like a 'creel' or basket. Balaam's ass in the Bible was unjustly beaten. Richard Martin's *Act to Prevent the Cruel and Improper Treatment of Cattle* was passed by Parliament in 1822. The Society for the Prevention of Cruelty to Animals was founded in 1824 and Queen Victoria permitted it to use the prefix 'Royal' from 1840. Bull-baiting, bear-baiting, badger-baiting, cock-fighting and dog-fighting were made illegal in 1835.

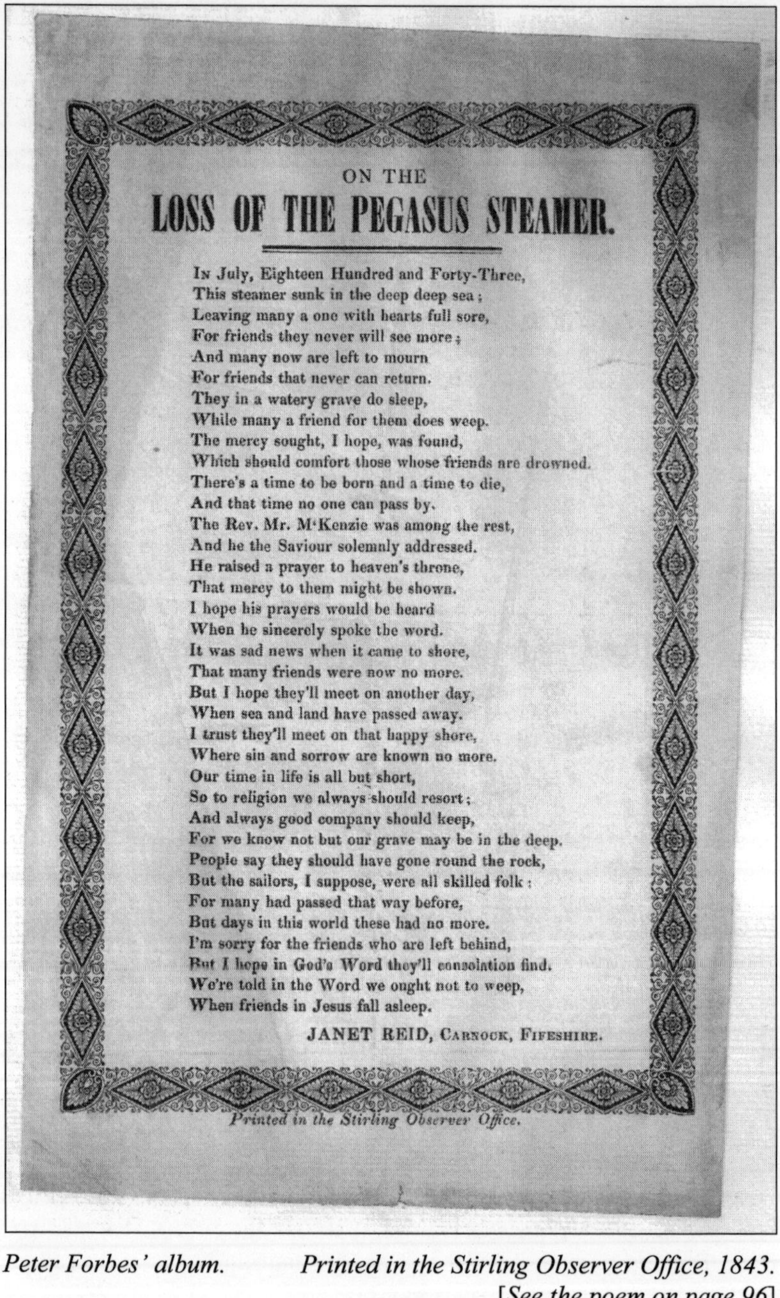

ON THE

LOSS OF THE PEGASUS STEAMER.

In July, Eighteen Hundred and Forty-Three,
This steamer sunk in the deep deep sea;
Leaving many a one with hearts full sore,
For friends they never will see more;
And many now are left to mourn
For friends that never can return.
They in a watery grave do sleep,
While many a friend for them does weep.
The mercy sought, I hope, was found,
Which should comfort those whose friends are drowned.
There's a time to be born and a time to die,
And that time no one can pass by.
The Rev. Mr. M'Kenzie was among the rest,
And he the Saviour solemnly addressed.
He raised a prayer to heaven's throne,
That mercy to them might be shown.
I hope his prayers would be heard
When he sincerely spoke the word.
It was sad news when it came to shore,
That many friends were now no more.
But I hope they'll meet on another day,
When sea and land have passed away.
I trust they'll meet on that happy shore,
Where sin and sorrow are known no more.
Our time in life is all but short,
So to religion we always should resort;
And always good company should keep,
For we know not but our grave may be in the deep.
People say they should have gone round the rock,
But the sailors, I suppose, were all skilled folk:
For many had passed that way before,
But days in this world these had no more.
I'm sorry for the friends who are left behind,
But I hope in God's Word they'll consolation find.
We're told in the Word we ought not to weep,
When friends in Jesus fall asleep.

JANET REID, Carnock, Fifeshire.

Printed in the Stirling Observer Office.

Peter Forbes' album. *Printed in the Stirling Observer Office, 1843.*

[*See the poem on page 96*]

Page 96: ON THE LOSS OF THE PEGASUS STEAMER

On the Loss of the Pegasus Steamer was composed by Janet Reid in Bridge of Allan soon after 20 July 1843. The broadside is one of nine printed in the Stirling Observer Office with Janet's home put as 'Carnock, Fifeshire' which were printed in the same batch and bought from her on a single occasion in 1843. They are now in Peter Forbes' album but not put together. The paddle-steamer *Pegasus* was built in 1835 for the Hull and Leith Steam Packet Company. The ship left Granton Harbour, Leith near Edinburgh, bound for Hull but struck the Goldstone Rock off the Farne Islands just after midnight on 20 July 1843. Twelve of the 16 crew and 51 of the 57 passengers were drowned including the Rev. J.M. Mackenzie. Ships going south could pass either to the east of the Longstone lighthouse and seaward of the Farne Islands; or they could take the Inner Passage leaving the Goldstone Rock buoy to port. Captain Alexander Miller took the Inner Passage but left the Goldstone Rock buoy to starboard and he was on the ship's bridge at the time. The inquest gave a verdict of: 'Accidental death occasioned by the gross carelessness of the master and those on lookout'.

Page 97: ON VAN AMBURGH'S EXHIBITION AT BRIDGE OF ALLAN

On Van Amburgh's Exhibition at Bridge of Allan was composed by Janet Reid soon after 8 September 1843. William M. Johnson writes online in *The Rose-Tinted Menagerie* (2007) that Isaac Van Amburgh (1801-1865) was an American showman from New York who by the age of 23 owned a travelling menagerie. He was the first man to introduce performing wild animals into the circus ring; the first man to enter a cage of jungle beasts in public; and the first man to put his head into a lion's mouth. His menagerie performed six times before an 'enthralled' Queen Victoria in 1838. By the mid-1840s Isaac Van Amburgh owned the largest travelling show in Britain. 'Mr Barr's Park' was next to Matthew Barr's Airthrey Wells Hotel in Bridge of Allan.

Page 99: ON THE YEAR 1844

On the Year 1844 was composed by Janet Reid at the beginning of 1844. The broadside has no printer's imprint but it can be deduced as printed by Macdonald in Edinburgh. It is the earliest broadside found with Janet Reid's home put as 'Bridge of Allan'.

Page 101: ON THE DISTRESS OF THE WORKING CLASSES

On the Distress of the Working Classes was composed by Janet Reid in 1844. The broadside has Janet Reid's home put 'Bridge of Allan' and it was printed by William Gilchrist at 145 Argyle Street, Glasgow, where he moved in 1844 according to the online *Scottish Book Trade Index*. Emigration from Scotland followed the Highland clearances in the early 1800s and the failure of the potato crop in the 1840s. Bridge of Allan is 15 miles west of Carnock! Janet probably put her home as Bridge of Allan from late in 1843.

Page 102: ON AN UNFORTUNATE LADY

On an Unfortunate Lady was composed by Janet Reid after reports of a divorce. The broadside was printed by William Gilchrist in 1844. Divorce in Scotland was obtainable through an Ecclesiastic Court since 1563 on the grounds of adultery or desertion. Divorce in England was obtainable only after separation by an Ecclesiastic Court and then divorce by a Private Act of Parliament.

Page 103: ON THE READING-ROOM

On the Reading-Room was composed by Janet Reid in Bridge of Allan in 1844, the year Major John Alexander Henderson (1806-1858) retired from the army. This 'Reading-Room' is the 'Tee-shaped', two-storey Reading-Room built by Major Henderson in 1842 on the corner of the future Henderson Street and Union Street. It is now named The Westerton Arms Hotel. The 'hand' on the sign was probably the Henderson clan crest: 'A dexter hand erect holding a star of six points wavy, surmounted by a crescent argent'. Leslie McGregor writes in the *Bridge of Allan Times* (Spring 2011) that the bowling-green on Union Street was laid out by Mr Barclay of the Mine House Tavern in 1840-41 for the 'Upper Bridge of Allan Bowling Club' which changed its name to the 'Well House Bowling Club' and then to the 'Airthrey Spa Bowling Club'.

Page 104: ON THE BONNY NEW CHURCH AT THE BRIDGE OF ALLAN

On the Bonny New Church at the Bridge of Allan was probably composed by Janet Reid in 1844 when the Free Church opened on the corner of Union Street and Keir Street in Bridge of Allan despite mention of 1843 when the foundation stone was laid. It became a school and it is now converted into flats as Drummond Cottage.

Page 105: ON THE OPENING OF THE NEW SCHOOL AT BRIDGE OF ALLAN

On the Opening of the New School at Bridge of Allan was composed by Janet Reid in Bridge of Allan soon after 4 November 1844 when the Free Church opened its first school in Market Street (now Fountain Road) in Bridge of Allan. The school moved into the first Free Church in 1854. The three ministers were probably the Rev. Peter W. Young, the Rev. Robert J. Johnstone and the Rev. John Ferguson. The 'Major' was Major John Alexander Henderson. 'Mr McRobie' was possibly Robert MacRobie who managed the Airthrey Paper Mills and died in 1852. 'Mr Wright' may have been Robert Wright or William Wright, both were wrights or joiners who had feued (leased) plots in Bridge of Allan in 1837 according to George Dixon in 'The Founding Decade of Modern Bridge of Allan, 1836-45' published in *The Forth Naturalist and Historian* (2004).

Page 107: MILSEY BANK FEMALE SCHOOL

Milsey Bank Female School was composed by Janet Reid when this school for infant girls opened in Lecropt, Bridge of Allan, probably about the same time as the new Free Church School opened in 1844. An infant school for boys was also opened nearby. Milsey Bank House was built in 1833 as a money-bank for the 10 mills – paper mills, meal mills and sawmills – on the Allan Water between Bridge of Allan and Dunblane. 'The worthy gentleman' was Archibald Stirling (1769-1847) the laird of Keir House in Lecropt.

Page 108: ON THE FARMERS

On the Farmers was composed by Janet Reid in Bridge of Allan most likely in 1845. Janet implies in this poem that she was once an 'agricultural labourer'. Women did all kinds of work on farms in Scotland except work with horses which was regarded as men's work. In the early 1800s half the male workers in the Lowlands of Scotland were ploughmen. Women's pay was about half men's pay so spinsters and widows had difficulty in earning a living-wage.

Page 109: ON THE GARDENERS

On the Gardeners was composed by Janet Reid in Bridge of Allan most likely in 1845. This poem is in Janet's chapbook *Poems on Various Subjects* (1846) a copy of which is in Glasgow University Library.

Page 110: ON THE SHOEMAKERS

On the Shoemakers was composed by Janet Reid in Bridge of Allan most likely in 1845 for it is in her chapbook printed in 1846. The first 16 lines of this poem are more or less a repeat of 16 other lines in Janet's earlier poem *On the Gallant Shoemakers* (1839). So this series of 'trades' poems may be the same series of 'gallant trades' poems ('gallant' meaning 'polite to women') that Janet composed in 1839 with changed titles and evolved wording. Janet did not keep an archive of her poems but relied on her memory.

Page 111: ON THE JOLLY TAILORS

On the Jolly Tailors was composed by Janet Reid in Bridge of Allan most likely in 1845. In this poem Janet describes how she was taught to read by a boy who became a tailor.

Page 113: ON THE FLESHERS

On the Fleshers was composed by Janet Reid most likely in 1845. Many of the Scots words spoken by Janet were probably transposed into English by her scribes, except those needed for rhyming and in the titles. Scots fell into disuse after the Union with England in 1707 and it was discouraged in Scottish schools.

Page 114: AGAINST SABBATH BREAKING

Against Sabbath Breaking was composed by Janet Reid in Bridge of Allan most likely in 1845. The broadside was printed in the Stirling Observer Office in 1846 with Janet's home put as 'Bridge of Allan' but without the double inverted commas for speech which are added for clarity in the version of this poem in her chapbook entitled *Poems on Various Subjects* (1846). This almost certainly indicates that the chapbook was printed later in 1846 than the broadside. This broadside is one of 11 broadsides, 10 of which were printed in the same batch after July 1846 (when Barr's Hotel re-opened for Janet's poem *On Barr's Bonny Hotel* is included in the chapbook). These 11 broadsides were almost certainly bought from Janet on one occasion by the same person in 1846 probably as a 'souvenir' of Bridge of Allan. They were once in the British Museum in London and are now in the British Library, London. The Trossachs is a scenic area in the Scottish Highlands. The Presbyterian Churches in Scotland strongly opposed working or pleasurable pursuits on the Sabbath (Sunday).

The 'Paraphrase [Bible]' is the Bible paraphrased, versed and put into a metre for singing to supplement the Psalter (Psalms) in Presbyterian churches. The singing of hymns and the playing of musical instruments was not permitted in the Established Church of Scotland or in the Free Church of Scotland at this time.

Page 116: ON A DAY OF HUMILIATION

On a Day of Humiliation was composed by Janet Reid possibly in 1845 for it is in her chapbook printed in 1846. Periodic days of 'Humiliation, Fasting and Prayer' had been held since 1690 after the Reformation. The General Assembly of the Church of Scotland appointed 22 July 1841 and 21 July 1842 as two such days: 'Being deeply impressed with the continued tokens of the Divine displeasure still resting on the Church and on this highly favoured and guilty land'. Dorcas in the Bible is a good woman.

Page 117: ON THE SEVENTH OF NOVEMBER or ON THE LOSS OF THE POTATOES

On the Seventh of November was composed by Janet Reid in Bridge of Allan on 7 November 1845 probably when challenged by a buyer to compose a poem on that day. The broadside of this poem is entitled *On the Seventh of November* but this poem in Janet's chapbook *Poems on Various Subjects* (1846) is retitled *On the Loss of the Potatoes*. The failure of the potato crop was due to a fungal blight that rotted the potatoes in the ground. *The Stirling Observer* on 16 and 30 October 1845 and on 6 November 1845 (the day before Janet composed this poem) reported that the potatoes newly lifted around Falkirk, Glasgow and Auchterarder were diseased. This blight caused the Highland Potato Famine (1846-57) which ruined the economy of the Highlands and Western Islands where potatoes and herrings were staple foods. It also caused the Great Irish Famine (1845-52).

Page 119: ON THE BONNY ALLEY TREE

On the Bonny Alley Tree was composed by Janet Reid in retrospect for her visit to Carnock Fair in May 1846 despite mention of 1838 in the poem. The words of this poem indicate that Janet first visited Bridge of Allan in 1841 and they also imply that she last visited Carnock in 1841. This interpretation accords with the record of Janet Reid staying in Torryburn near Carnock at the time of the national census on 6-7 June 1841.

Page 120: ON THE REV. MR BRAND'S DEATH, IN DUNFERMLINE

On the Rev. Mr Brand's Death, in Dunfermline was composed by Janet Reid in retrospect for sale as a broadside at Carnock Fair in May 1846 despite mention of 1838 in the poem. The Rev. George Bell Brand (1786-1838) the minister of St Andrew's Church, Dunfermline, died on 21 February 1838. The old form of address 'Rev. Mr' used by Janet is the form used in *The 'Old' Statistical Account of Scotland* (compiled 1791-1799). Fossoway Church is 7 miles north of Carnock and Torryburn Church is on the shore of the Firth of Forth 2 miles south of Carnock.

Page 121: ON A PLEASANT YOUNG GENTLEMAN

On a Pleasant Young Gentleman was composed by Janet Reid probably in 1846. The 'Gentleman' in Blair House was Alexander Allison who began mining iron-ore in 1845 and built the Forth Iron Works in 1846 which closed in 1869. The 'lady' in Blair House before him was Mrs Mill whose husband George Mill owned Blair Colliery, Carnock. This 'beloved minister' is probably the Rev. William Gilston (1792-1881) who is buried in the Old Kirkyard.

Page 123: ON GLASGOW'S BONNY CITY (a new poem with a reused title)

On Glasgow's Bonny City was composed by Janet Reid in Bridge of Allan probably in 1846. This is a new poem which reuses an old title of Janet's earlier poem composed in Glasgow in 1840. 'The Cross' is where High Street, Gallowgate, London Road, Saltmarket and Trongate meet and a Market Cross stood there until it was removed in 1659 after the Reformation. An equestrian statue of King William III (1650-1702) was erected in Trongate in 1735: 'In commemoration of the Glorious Revolution of 1688-89'. Soldiers wore red uniforms – Janet liked red clothing!

Page 125: ON BARR'S BONNY HOTEL

On Barr's Bonny Hotel was composed by Janet Reid soon after The Airthrey Wells Hotel reopened on Wednesday 15 July 1846. The broadside was printed in the Stirling Observer Office in 1846. In 1848 the Scottish Central Railway reached Perth via Stirling and Bridge of Allan and by the early 1850s over 30,000 visitors were arriving annually in Bridge of Allan most of them by rail.

Page 127: ON PHILP'S BONNY ROYAL HOTEL

On Philp's Bonny Royal Hotel was composed by Janet Reid in Bridge of Allan most likely in 1846 at the same time as she composed *On Barr's Bonny Hotel.*

Pages 128 & 129: POEMS ON VARIOUS SUBJECTS

Poems on Various Subjects is the title of Janet Reid's chapbook privately published in Bridge of Allan and printed in the Stirling Observer Office and dated 1846. It is a little less than half the size of her broadsides and it was printed on a single sheet of paper, folded to give eighteen leaves or thirty-six pages. It contains 34 poems in no particular order of which 13 have not been found as broadsides. This chapbook was evidently published in 1846 after she composed *On Barr's Bonny Hotel*. Janet probably gave the printer 34 broadsides of the poems to copy that she had to hand (including *On the Year Forty-Two*) so these poems were in relatively recent use.

Page 131: ON A JACK-DAW,
ON THE BANKS OF THE ALLAN

On a Jack-Daw, On the Banks of the Allan was composed by Janet Reid probably about 1850. The original title was probably 'On a Jackdaw' and it was later suffixed by 'On the Banks of the Allan' to associate it with the song 'On the Banks of Allan Water' (1812) by Matthew Gregory 'Monk' Lewis to attract more buyers. Janet (or the printer) may also have substituted 'Water' instead of 'Bridge' in the fourth line of this printing. This 'Mr Stirling' is William, later Sir William (1817-1888), the son of Archibald Stirling. The Rumbling Brig and the Cauthrin Linn (cauldrons waterfalls) are on the River Devon 13 miles north-east of Bridge of Allan.

Page 133: ON THE YEAR 1853

On the Year 1853 was composed by Janet Reid at the beginning of that year. The Church of Scotland recognised only the Sabbath day (Sunday) as holy for Saint's Days and Christmas Day had no Biblical authority. Hogmanay (the last day of the year) and New Year's Day became the focus of popular celebrations in Scotland. Janet probably composed a poem for every New Year, but only those for 1841, 1842, 1843, 1844 and 1853 have been found.

On Pretty Paisley.

THE people of Glasgow and Paisley are very smart,
They can bring in meal and potatoes without horse or cart,
If people in my young days had been so smart
They would have sworn over them they had the black art;
It's a great pleasure to see the bonnie coaches reek;
But it is a cruel thing to see men the poor horses for to whip;
It surely was a good invention
Who of the railway first did mention,
If people have money and time to spare
They soon can go as far as Air,
And if they have to hurry back,
The railway brings them in a crack;
If the poor have a sixpence, they cannot be beat,
For they can get in the Coach altho' it has not seat,
It is a great convenience for both rich and poor,
I hope it will be a long time e'er it be given o'er.
All earthly works must drop at the last day,
And I hope Paisley folks will near forget to pray,
When in Paisley I was in a praying house,
With a respectable woman both sober and douse,
I went three times to church on Sabbath day,
And neighbours met at night with them to pray;
As long's I live I will remember
I went to pretty Paisley on the 15th of September.
I hope Paisley people ever will advise
The young and youthful to be wise,
And may they spend their days in grace,
And may their latter end be peace.

JANET REID, *Carnock.*

Graham, Printer.

Peter Forbes' album. *Printed by Thomas Graham, Paisley, 1842.*
[*See the poem on page 57*]

A CHECKLIST OF JANET REID'S POEMS

JANET REID'S poems are listed in a chronological order under the year of composition which is also the year of their first printing.

Janet frequently changes her poems. She changes words, phrases or lines; adds lines, switches lines or omits lines; and she changes titles. The transcriptions are based upon the earliest version found except where later changes clarify the meaning. Additional lines found in the later printings are inserted; and earlier lines that are later found omitted are retained. Such combinations may have been printed.

Her scribes and printers had a free hand. The most typical of the many variations found are reproduced – but some consistency is introduced. Line-breaks are used when there is not enough space for the full line – that being the principle used by Janet's printers.

The title of a poem is suffixed by any '(date)' given in the poem or any '[date]' of an event that can be dated which may indicate the date of composition. These are followed by the source (indicated by Key letters) and Janet's home indicated as put on the broadside:

Ca	Carnock
CF	Carnock, Fifeshire
BA	Bridge of Allan

followed by the printer and the printer's flowers (also indicated by Key letters) and the attributed year for each printing.

A 'year' of printing indicates that a date is put on the broadside by the printer or a contemporary date is annotated or it is one of Janet Reid's 'New Year' poems.

A '[year]' of printing indicates that no date is given in the poem or no event is given that can be dated (or the broadside is evidently a later printing) but a date can be attributed from other evidence.

A '[year?]' of printing indicates that no date is given in the poem or no event is given that can be dated (or the broadside is evidently a later printing) but a year is assumed which is probably correct.

A 'year#' of printing indicates that it is one of three batches of broadsides (1842#, 1843# or 1846#) printed at the same time by The Stirling Observer Office for which the year of printing of at least one broadside in each batch is known or can be deduced.

Key Letters indicating the Sources:

BL British Library, London:

a 11 broadsides bound together and acquired before 1901.

b 2 broadsides in an album entitled *Poetical Scrap Book* (one of three albums of cuttings about women authors) collected by the Rev. Francis John Stainforth and acquired in 1868 but only catalogued in recent years.

D Dunfermline Carnegie Library: 11 broadsides collected before 1901 and given by Erskine Beveridge (1853-1920) as part of his collection of books and now mounted on boards.

G Glasgow University Library: a chapbook entitled *Poems on Various Subjects* (1846) by Janet Reid containing 34 poems privately published by her and printed in the Stirling Observer Office, collected and given by David Murray in 1927.

M Mitchell Library, Glasgow: 9 broadsides collected in the 1850s and bound together as '*Some of the Works of Janet Reid, the Bridge of Allan Poetess, Native of Carnock, Fifeshire*'.

NLS National Library of Scotland, Edinburgh:

a 1 broadside acquired post 1975.

b 1 broadside in an album entitled *Street Literature* collected by William Harvey (1874-1936) and acquired in 1979. This broadside was put online by the NLS in 2004 among 1,800 broadsides under *The Word on the Street – Broadsides*.

PF Peter Forbes' album, Stirling County Archives: 35 broadsides mounted in an album entitled *Rhymes by Janet Reid, Carnock* found by David A. Flint in D.M. Beach's in Salisbury in 1998. In 2010 it was given to the Dr William Halliday Welsh Educational and Historical Trust collection in Bridge of Allan which since 2012 is kept in the Stirling County Archives.

W Wellcome Library for the History & Understanding of Medicine, London: 1 broadside appended (by accident) to a disbound 28-page leaflet entitled *Observations on Cerebral and Spinal Apoplexy, Paralysis, and Convulsions of New-Born Infants* by Evory Kennedy (Dublin: 1836).

Key Letters indicating the Printers:

These printers in Dunfermline are named by Erskine Beveridge in *A Bibliography of Works Relating to Dunfermline and the West of Fife* (1901) but no broadsides were found printed by them:

- John Miller: Abbey Park Place (1805); 9 Bridge Street (1806-1835) and as John Miller & Son (1835-1866).
- William Clark: 46 High Street (1840-1868).
- William Meldrun: Nethertown (1813-1844).

Details of these printers come from the *Scottish Book Trade Index*, an online resource of the National Library of Scotland, Edinburgh:

hb Hugh Baird: 174 Trongate, Glasgow.
wg William Gilchrist: 99 Trongate, Glasgow (1840); 11 St Enoch Square, Glasgow (by 1844); and 145 Argyll Street, Glasgow (1844-1887).
ma Macdonald comprising John Macdonald, Mrs Macdonald, William James Macdonald and H. Macdonald: 13 Carrubbers' Close (1833-1860).
jn John Neilson: 15 St Mirren's Court, Paisley (1834); 15 St Mirren's Street, Paisley (1838); and 101 High Street, Paisley (to 1852).
tg Thomas Graham: possibly originally in business on his own, he became a partner of John Neilsen and he took over John Neilsen's business in 1852.
so Stirling Observer Office: 38 Baker Street, Stirling (1836-1843); and 22-23 Murray Place, Stirling (1843-1880).
[np] no printer's imprint – where the printer can be deduced the printer is also indicated within the square brackets.

Broadsides printed in the Stirling Observer Office use different type-cases for the printer's imprint which are further designated:

Up Upper case: PRINTED IN THE STIRLING OBSERVER OFFICE.
It Italic case: *Printed in the Stirling Observer Office.*
Tc Title-case: Printed in the Stirling Observer Office.

The choice of type-case may have been the printer's policy at the time (there are insufficient survivals to know) or it may have been the whim of the printer. However, use of the same type-case can be used to deduce which broadsides were printed in the same batch.

Key Letters indicating the Printer's Flowers:

Early printers' ornaments were cast in the shape of flowers or leaves – hence their typographical name 'fleurons' or 'printer's flowers'. This ❧ (a hedera or ivy leaf) is the earliest one from circa 1500. Printer's flowers are pieces of type and they are used repetitively as borders on Janet Reid's broadsides but not on her chapbook. Those on Janet's broadsides are designated by a '(letter)' in the alphabetical order in which they were found to be chronologically used:

(a) Unknown printer [Kirkcaldy ?]

(b) Unknown printer [Edinburgh ?]

[Though the style of (b) is similar to (f), the typeface used by this unknown printer is different to that used by Hugh Baird in Glasgow]

(c) Macdonald, Edinburgh

(d) Macdonald, Edinburgh

(e) Macdonald, Edinburgh [type (c) rearranged]

(f) Hugh Baird, Glasgow

(f) Hugh Baird, Glasgow

(h) Hugh Baird, Glasgow

(i) John Neilson, Paisley

(j) Thomas Graham, Paisley

(k) Thomas Graham, Paisley

(l) Unknown printer [Falkirk ?]

(m) Hugh Gilchrist, Glasgow

(n) Hugh Gilchrist, Glasgow

(o) Hugh Gilchrist, Glasgow [type (n) rearranged]

(p) Hugh Gilchrist, Glasgow

(q) Hugh Gilchrist, Glasgow

(r) Stirling Observer Office

(s) Stirling Observer Office [type (r) rearranged]

The broadside of *On Edinburgh City* printed in the Stirling Observer Office in 1846 (which is one of a batch of 10 poems printed at the same time) has the printer's flowers arranged as 'dog-teeth' (s) in three of the borders and as 'diamonds' (r) in the bottom border – evidently by mistake. So the arrangement of the printers' flowers was almost certainly at the whim of the printer and the use of the same printer's flowers or the same arrangement of them cannot be used to date the broadsides – but they can be used to identify the printer of a broadside or to deduce which broadsides were printed in the same batch.

Janet Reid may have been inspired to use printer's flowers by their frequent use on religious tracts. The printer would have typeset each poem afresh each time Janet came with a batch of her poems for printing (printers were always short of type at this time). But the printer almost certainly kept the printers' flowers and the printer's imprint as already set-up for the previous broadside in the batch when type-setting the next poem in the batch.

A Checklist of Janet Reid's Poems:

Title | Date(s) in the Poem: Key Letters | Date of Printing(s)

1837:

On the Honourable Manufacturers of Dunfermline [1837]:
D Ca [np] (b) [1840?]
On the Spring [no date]: **PF** Ca hb (h) [1840]
PF Ca wg (n) [1842]
M Ca wg (n) [1842]
PF CF so *It* (r) 1843 #
G so 1846
Lament for a Beloved Minister [1837]: **PF** Ca hb (b) [1840]

1838:

On a Comfortable Cup of Tea [no date]: **NLSb** Ca ma (d) [1840?]
PF Ca jn (i) [1840?]
M Ca wg (n) 24th edition March 1842 (footnote)
D CF so UP (s) 26th edition 1842#
BLa BA so UP (s) 32nd edition 1846 #
G so 1846
On Children Going to Church [no date]:
PF CF so *It* (r) 15th edn. 1843 #
G so 1846
On Humility [no date]:
PF & **M** (duplicates) Ca tg (k) 11th edn. [1842]
D CF so UP (s) 13th edition 1842#
BLa BA so UP (s) 17th edition 1846 #
G so 1846

1839:

On Giving Work to Working Folk [no date]: **PF** Ca hb (h) [1840]
On Cruel Murder [no date]: **W** Ca ma (c) [1840?]
On the Gallant Sailors [1839]: **PF** Ca [np] (a) [1839?]
M Ca wg (m) [1842]
D CF so UP (s) 1842#
G so 1846
On the Gallant Shoemakers (1839): **PF** Ca hb (g) [1840]

1840:

On the Mid-Mill (1840): **PF** Ca hb (h) 1840 (handwritten note)

On Glasgow, Bonny Town (1840): **PF** Ca hb (h) [1840]
or *On Glasgow's Bonny City* (a change in title):
PF Ca wg (n) 7th edition April 1842 (footnote)
D CF so UP (s) 8th edition 1842 #
On Pretty Paisley (1st September) [1840]: **PF** Ca tg (j) [1842?]

1841:
On the Year 1841 (1 January 1841): **NLSa** Ca [np] (l) 1841
On Airthrey Water [no date]: **PF** CF so *It* (r) 1843#
G so 1846
On Dunblane [no date]: **M** Ca wg (m) 1842 (footnote)
In Speaking Be Mild [no date]: **PF** Ca tg (j) [1842?]

1842:
On the Year Forty-Two (1 January 1842): **G** so 1846
Melancholy Accident (21 March 1842):
PF & **M** (duplicates) Ca wg (n) [1842]
Against Sabbath Breakers [21 February 1842]:
PF & **M** (duplicates) Ca wg (o) April 1842 (footnote)
On Airthrey Well House [1842]: **PF** CF so *It* (r) 1843#
On The Bonny Brig o' Allan [1842]: **PF** CF wg (n) [1843]
G so 1846
BLb BA so Tc (s) [1850?]
For Young Ladies [no date]: **D** CF so UP (s) 1842#
PF CF so *It* (r) 1843#
For Gentlemen and Ladies [no date]: **PF** CF so *It* (r) 1843#
or *For Ladies and Gentlemen* (a change in title):
BLa BA so UP (s) 1846#
G so 1846
For Bachelors [no date]: **D** CF so UP (s) 1842#
BLa BA so UP (s) 1846#
G so 1846
On an Accident at the Brig o' Allan (18 June 1842):
D CF so UP (s) 1842#
On Vanity Fair (6 August 1842): **D** CF so UP (s) 1842#
G so 1846
On Drapers and Grocers [29 August 1842]: **PF** CF wg (m) [1843]
A Check for Scoffers [1 September1842]: **D** CF so UP (s) 1842#
PF CF [np ma] (e) [1843]
G so 1846

Title | Date(s) in the Poem: Key Letters | Date of Printing(s)

The Queen's Farewell (13 September 1842): **D** CF so UP (s) 1842#
PF CF so *It* (r) 1843#
BLa BA so UP (s) 1846#
G so 1846

1843:
For the New-Year (1 January 1843): **PF** CF wg (n) 1843
On the Faithful Ministers of the Church of Scotland [January 1843]:
PF CF wg (n) [1843]
On Respectable Bakers [no date]: **PF** CF [np ma] (e) [1843]
On Edinburgh City [21 February 1842]: **PF** CF ma (e) [1843]
BLa BA so UP (r and s) 1846 #
G so 1846
Be Merciful to Body and to Beast [no date]: **PF** CF so *It* (r) 1843#
G so 1846
On the Loss of the Pegasus Steamer (20 July 1843):
PF CF *It* so (r) 1843#
G so 1846
On Van Amburgh's Exhibition at Bridge of Allan (8th September 1843): **M** CF so *It* (s) [1843]

1844:
On the Year 1844 (1 January 1844): **PF** BA [np ma] (e) 1844
On the Distress of the Working Classes [no date]:
PF BA wg (p) [1844]
G so 1846
On an Unfortunate Lady [no date]: **PF** BA wg (q) [1844]
On the Reading-Room [1842, 1844]: **G** so 1846
On the Bonny New Church at the Bridge of Allan (1843) [1844]:
G so 1846
On the Opening of the New School at Bridge of Allan (4 November 1844): **G** so 1846
Milsey Bank Female School [1844]: **PF** BA so UP (s) [1844]

1845:
On the Farmers [no date]: **G** so 1846
On the Gardeners [no date]: **G** so 1846
On the Shoemakers [no date]: **G** so 1846
On the Jolly Tailors [no date]: **G** so 1846

On the Fleshers [no date]: **G** so 1846
Against Sabbath Breaking [no date]: **BLa** BA so UP (s) 1846#
G so 1846
On a Day of Humiliation [22 July 1841 or 21 July 1842]: **G** so 1846
On the Seventh of November (7 November 1845):
BLa BA so UP (r) [1846]
or *On the Loss of the Potatoes* (a change in title): **G** so 1846

1846:
On the Bonny Alley Tree (1838 in retrospect) [1846]: **G** so 1846
On the Rev. Mr Brand's Death, in Dunfermline (1838 in retrospect):
G so 1846
On a Pleasant Young Gentleman [1846]: **G** so 1846
On Glasgow's Bonny City (a new poem with a re-used title)
[no date]: **BLa** BA so UP (s) 1846#
G so 1846
On Barr's Bonny Hotel [15th July] (1846): **BLa** BA so UP (s) 1846#
G so 1846
On Philp's Bonny Royal Hotel [1846]: **BLa** BA so UP (s) 1846#
G so 1846
Poems on Various Subjects (a chapbook of 34 poems all listed here as source **G** so 1846) Stirling 1846: **G** BA so 1846

1850:
On a Jack-daw, on The Banks of The Allan [no date]:
BLb BA so Tc (r) [1850?]

1853:
On the Year 1853 (1 January 1853): **M** BA so Tc (r) (1853)

[And many more …]

Every broadside found by Janet Reid and her chapbook is listed here. This listing, arranged in a slightly different chronological order, was first published in 'Janet Reid (1777-1854): Forgotten Poetess of Carnock and Bridge of Allan' in *The Forth Naturalist and Historian*, University of Stirling, Volume 32: 2009. The above order is subject to further review if any new broadsides are found.

ACKNOWLEDGEMENTS

IN this Quest for Janet Reid, I visited every library that holds her broadsides and her chapbook and they provided copies for which I am grateful. I visited almost every village and town that Janet did and searched five graveyards where she may have been buried.

I would like to thank all those who have helped me, in particular J. Malcolm Allan of Bridge of Allan, Christopher Neale (formerly of Dunfermline Carnegie Library), Morna Daniels (formerly of the British Library), John Henderson (formerly of Stirling) now of Cyprus, Lizz Mogg of Carnock and the late Roger B. Flint.

The quotation from *The History of Street Literature* (1973) by Leslie Shepard is by courtesy of David & Charles Ltd.

The broadside of *On the Honourable Manufacturers of Dunfermline* is reproduced by courtesy of Dunfermline Carnegie Library, Fife Council Libraries and Museums.

The broadside of *On Cruel Murder* is reproduced by courtesy of the Librarian, Wellcome Library for the History & Understanding of Medicine, London.

The broadside of *On the Year 1841* is reproduced by permission of The Trustees of the National Library of Scotland.

The broadside of *On Dunblane* is reproduced by courtesy of the Mitchell Library, Glasgow.

The front of the chapbook entitled *Poems on Various Subjects* (1846) by Janet Reid is reproduced by courtesy of the Department of Special Collections, University of Glasgow Library.

David A. Flint

Further information would be welcomed about Janet Reid or about new sources of her poems or broadsides. Please contact me at:

30 Barn Lane, Oakley, Basingstoke RG23 7HT
davidaflint@btinternet.com
01256 781413